Aboard a Dutch Troop Transport
En Route to South Africa
1802

A
Diary
Written
by
Captain Ludwig Alberti
of the
Waldeck 5th Battalion

During the Voyage of the 5th Waldeck Battalion from Alkmaar in North Holland to the Cape of Good Hope and During the Unit's Stay There

Translated from German
by
Bruce E. Burgoyne

HERITAGE BOOKS
2008

HERITAGE BOOKS
AN IMPRINT OF HERITAGE BOOKS, INC.

Books, CDs, and more—Worldwide

For our listing of thousands of titles see our website
at
www.HeritageBooks.com

Published 2008 by
HERITAGE BOOKS, INC.
Publishing Division
100 Railroad Ave. #104
Westminster, Maryland 21157

Copyright © 2008 Bruce E. Burgoyne

All rights reserved. No part of this book may be reproduced or transmitted in any form or by any means, electronic or mechanical, including photocopying, recording or by any information storage and retrieval system without written permission from the author, except for the inclusion of brief quotations in a review.

International Standard Book Numbers
Paperbound: 978-0-7884-4544-6
Clothbound: 978-0-7884-7718-8

Aboard a Dutch Troop Transport
en route to South Africa, 1802

Introduction

My friend, Ingeborg Moldenhauer, archivist of the Waldeck Historical Society, gave me a typed, German language copy of the diary of Captain Ludwig Alberti's travels from Holland to the Cape of Good Hope in 1802. Alberti, born 1767 or 1768 in Pyrmont, sailed as captain commandant of the Colonel's Company of the 5th Waldeck Battalion in the service of the Batavian Republic [Holland]. He then served at the Cape as commander of the Jaeger Company of the battalion, due to promotions and transfers resulting from the death of Colonel Friederich von Wilmowsky while *en route* to the Cape. Although this portion of the diary covers only the voyage to the Cape, the actual diary may be longer, as indicated by the title. In addition to ship-board life, Alberti describes visits in Lisbon and the Canary Islands, and marine life witnessed along the way.

There are errors in the German version,

Aboard a Dutch Troop Transport
en route to South Africa, 1802

possibly made when copying from the original, or when making a typed copy. Most noticeable of these are in the description of watches aboard ship [under date of 6 August]. And the explanation of the amount of water used [under date of 6 December].

Also, the reader should note that distances, temperatures, and location figures may vary as measurements are given, apparently sometimes in English miles, sometimes in German miles. One German mile equals six English miles, and as a rule, one German hour equals three English miles. Temperature readings appear to be in Fahrenheit.

There are, I am sure, mistakes in the English translation, also. One obvious area of disagreement may be in my use of 'boatman fish" instead of 'pilot fish' [under date of 27 October]. However, none of the errors, in the German version or my translation, appear to alter Captain Alberti's interesting account, which is an excellent companion piece to the *Lijsten Boek voor 't 5de Battalion Waldeck,* also

Aboard a Dutch Troop Transport
en route to South Africa, 1802

in the Waldeck Historical Society. The *Lijsten Boek* contains monthly unit rosters [1802-06].

Finally, I should point out that the 5th Battalion is a later designation of the 3rd English-Waldeck Regiment, which fought for England against the American colonists from 1776 to 1783, and some of the men were still in the unit when it sailed for the Cape of Good Hope.

I have divided the account into a number of sections to make for easier reading.

Bruce E. Burgoyne
Dover, DE
19 July 1987

Aboard a Dutch Troop Transport
en route to South Africa, 1802

1

Only the prompting of my conscience and the fulfillment of my promises to my most sincerely loved mother, brothers and sisters, and other close relatives, that I would provide them with an account of my experiences during this voyage and the related consequences, prompted me to keep this diary. Also, I am convinced that I have nothing to fear from my relatives if the presentation has any literary shortcomings. Further, my loved ones should not refuse their indulgence, if the necessary previous knowledge should fail me in making comments about subjects where my opinion is positively necessary, and which, in order not to misjudge, I therefore would prefer not to treat. On the other hand, I will adhere strictly to the truth and tell nothing of which I am not fully convinced is true.

The determination, as a result of the return of the Cape of Good Hope to the Batavian Republic by England, according to the terms of the Peace of Amiens, to enter into a treaty with

Aboard a Dutch Troop Transport *en route* to South Africa, 1802

His Serene Highness the Prince of Waldeck by the Batavian Republic, provided an agreement to send the 5th Battalion to the Cape of Good Hope. According to the treaty, the battalion was augmented and raised to the following strength, for which each of the other four battalions provided volunteers.

Staff

1 Lieutenant Colonel
1 Major
1 Adjutant
1 Regt Surgeon
1 Chaplain
1 Regt Drummer
5 Hautboists
2 Medical Assts
1 Gunsmith
14 Men

A Company of Jaegers

1 Captain
1 1st Lieutenant
1 2nd Lieutenant
4 Sergeants
1 Captain at arms
8 Corporals
2 Huntinghorn Players
96 Jaegers
114 Men

[Continued on next page]

Aboard a Dutch Troop Transport *en route* to South Africa, 1802

Strength of each of Six Companies of Fusiliers

1 Captain
1 1st Lieutenant
1 2nd Lieutenant
3 Sergeants
1 Captain at arms
6 Corporals
2 Drummers
<u>60</u> Fusiliers
75 Men

Later, each of the two staff companies were assigned a captain commandant, so that thereafter the battalion had a total strength of 580 men. To make the music more complete, in addition to the five hautboists, nine others were added, part of whom were carried on the company rolls as jaegers or fusiliers, part paid from a fund to which all officers had to contribute according to their rank.

The fusilier companies are numbered

Aboard a Dutch Troop Transport
en route to South Africa, 1802

according to the position in which they are arranged by the date of rank of their commanders within the battalion.

The following list contains the assignment and names of the complete officer corps at that time, by the date of rank, and company.

<u>Number of the Company</u>

1. Lieutenant Colonel
   [Friederich] von Wilmowsky   4
2. Major [Karl] Mueller   5
3. Captain [Karl] Gilten   Jaeger
4. Captain [Friederich] von Horn 6
5. Captain [Franz] Wirths   1
6. Captain [Bernhard] Schreiner   3
7. Captain [Friederich] Mueller   2
8. Captain Commandant
   [Wilhelm] Alberti   4
9. Captain Commandant
   [Daniel] Suden   5
10. 1st Lieutenant [?] Neumeyer 2
11. 1st Lieutenant [Ludwig]
    Alberti   Jaeger

Aboard a Dutch Troop Transport
en route to South Africa, 1802

		Number of the Company
12.	1st Lieutenant [Ludwig] Deppe	5
13.	1st Lieutenant [Casimir] Goette	4
14.	Quartermaster [Ernst] Neumeyer	Staff
15.	Adjutant [Friederich] Stoekker	Staff
16.	1st Lieutenant [August] Egger]	1
17.	1st Lieutenant [Ludwig] Von Breitenstein	6
18.	1st Lieutenant [August] Frensdorf	3
19.	2nd Lieutenant [Friederich] Ostheiden	2
20.	2nd Lieutenant [Karl] Mattern	Jaeger
21.	2nd Lieutenant [Ernst] Staudinger	1
22.	2nd Lieutenant [Benjamin] Reiss	3
23.	2nd Lieutenant [N.] Thirton	5
24.	2nd Lieutenant [Alexander] Klapp	4
25.	2nd Lieutenant [Franz] Gossinet [or Goffinet]	6
26.	Regt. Surgeon [F.] Wehr	Staff
27.	Chaplain [Henrich] Sproe [or Spror]	Staff

Of these officers, those who are married are

Aboard a Dutch Troop Transport
en route to South Africa, 1802

Lieutenant Colonel Wilmowsky and Captains Horn and Suden.

All officers of the troops which are assigned to the Cape of Good Hope or East or West Indies, received from the government, according to their rank, a bonus which amounts to 400 florin for a staff officer, 300 florin for a captain, and 200 florin for a subaltern. In addition, everyone, from the lieutenant colonel to the fusiliers, and down, received an advance of three months pay, which by the corporals and lower grades of the battalion is only partially given to them, and the remainder is withheld so that they can buy smoking and chewing tobacco and other such necessities during the voyage, because otherwise it is feared that a careless disposal of their money would prevent acquiring those items. Further, the battalion provided all required clothing for them for two years.

Aboard a Dutch Troop Transport *en route* to South Africa, 1802

2

Finally, the battalion received orders to march to Den Helder, in order to embark there, which followed under the direction of Major Mueller, as Lieutenant Colonel von Wilmowsky had received permission from the government to remain behind for a time because of personal affairs.

<u>1802, July 12, 13, and 14</u> - We marched from Alkmaar in North Holland to Schlagen and entered Den Helder, where we were embarked. When the idea of a long sea voyage and the great distance which the battalion would be from the fatherland is taken into account, it was certainly not strange that at the end of the battalion's stay in Alkmaar, and during the march to the embarkation, there were many desertions to be expected. However, a discipline based on reason and fairness, and a trust imbued in the conduct of the officers toward their subordinates, was such that the battalion lost only four men during the last days in Alkmaar, and not a single one later, on the

Aboard a Dutch Troop Transport
en route to South Africa, 1802

march.

The ships assigned to the transport of the troops and their baggage were divided into three divisions, of which the first consists of the *Pluto,* 70 guns, commanded by Schout bez. Nagt Dekker [or Dekler, hereafter translated as the commodore], the *Bato,* 28 guns, commanded by Captain Seegers, and the frigate *Maria Reigersbergen,* 32 guns, commanded by Captain Lambert. [The *Kartmaar, also spelled Kortmaar and Kortmamm,* may have been accidentally omitted by the person making the manuscript copy.] This division, as well as the other two composed of transport ships, was grouped together and convoyed by the corvettes the *Spy* [or *Spion*], Captain Sickema, and the *Fly* [Fliege], Captain Arkonbout, all under the orders of the commodore, and are to sail out, one after the other. After the troops have arrived at the Cape, almost all of the ships are to proceed to Batavia and take on sugar, etc., at that place. Because of this, and in order to take more troops on board, the ships of the line,

Aboard a Dutch Troop Transport
en route to South Africa, 1802

Pluto, Bato, and *Kartmaar,* are only partially armed and the lower row of cannons have been removed.

The Jaegers and the 1st, 2nd, 3rd, and 4th Companies of Fusiliers were embarked on the Kartmaar. Other than those, in the ships of the 1st division, there were two companies of light dragoons, one company of jaegers, and a company of artillery. On the *Bato* were embarked Commissary General de Mitt [also spelled de Mist and de Nist in the manuscript], who will take over the Cape from the English in the name of the government, and who will then establish the necessary administration, and Governor General Jansens, with their parties. They have the battalion's musicians with them.

All of the mentioned warships, as they are not on a war footing,, have only half of their usual crew on board.

The *Pluto*'s crew consists of 233 men   233

Five companies of the battalion, with wives and

Aboard a Dutch Troop Transport *en route* to South Africa, 1802

Children,   438
  Passengers, with their
wives and children,   12
make a total on the *Pluto* of   683 persons

Among the passengers are twenty men and Hedding, Justice Counsellor for the Cape, Kloete, Staff Officers [Untermajor] Frey and Morres, who belong to the Commissary General's party, and von Bickefeld, who is going to Batavia as a merchant [Unterkaufmann]. The naval officers are Captain-Lieutenant von der Fande, Lieutenant Pfeil, von Devender, Fredericks von der Burg, von Laken de Witt, van Barneveld, and van Feldern, Dr. Grossart [?-20 Grossart in the manuscript], and the ship's secretary Schotte.

The non-commissioned officers and privates of the battalion are quartered in the middle deck and assigned in so-called mess [Backs], of which each consists of a non-commissioned officer and fourteen privates. The officers are quartered four and four together in a cabin, and the captains, adjutant, and quartermaster under

Aboard a Dutch Troop Transport
en route to South Africa, 1802

the quarterdeck; the subalterns, however, between decks, and Major Mueller alone in a cabin on the quarterdeck. The cabins under the quarterdeck are six paces in width and breath, and those in between decks, even smaller. Each officer, non-commissioned officer, and private received a hammock, in which there is a mattress and a pillow filled with woolen cloth, as well as a woolen blanket. Most of the officers have provided themselves with a so-called "Kottra", which serves as a field bed. A "Kottra" is a type of hammock which is about six feet long, a bit more than two feet wide, and two feet deep. On the bottom is a wooden frame covered with linen, through which the shape of the "Kottra", when it is hung up, can be seen. It is much airier and comfortable than lying in the usual hammock, but naturally takes a much greater space than the others, also.

The following procedures are used to insure that the land troops and the seamen are given equal treatment. From Major Mueller to, and including the privates, each receives every

Aboard a Dutch Troop Transport
en route to South Africa, 1802

week, four pounds of ship's zwieback, one pound of cheese, and a half pound of butter. The wives of the non-commissioned officers draw an equal amount, but their children receive only half portions. All officers receive the noon meal, at government expense. After one o'clock the naval officers eat in the chapel, at three o'clock the captains and subalterns of the battalion follow them, and at about four o'clock the commodore and his guests, among which are the battalion staff officers, and the justice councilor, and a few other passengers. The latter, for whom the commodore pays, dine in the cabins. Except for those who dine with the commodore, each receives a half bottle of wine with their meal. For breakfast and other necessities, the individuals must generally provide for themselves. The non-commissioned officers and privates receive groats for breakfast, into which they put a part of their butter ration, or on Sunday and Thursday they receive a half pound of bacon and gray peas; on Tuesday, salted beef and gray

Aboard a Dutch Troop Transport
en route to South Africa, 1802

peas or sauerkraut, at which time, when the latter is issued, bacon instead of beef, which is then issued on another day. On the remaining days, normally, only yellow peas are served. The evening fare always consists of the same type of peas as were served at midday. Meat or bacon is put in the peas, or bacon is cooked in the peas, or the sauerkraut and these vegetables are seasoned therewith. On the days when only peas are served, however, the troops must season the vegetables with the bacon they have been able to save or with their own butter. Sundays and Tuesdays each man receives a seventh bottle of vinegar, which is issued to each Back or mess. Of all of this, the women and children receive a full and a half portion, also, and further, the groats, peas, and sauerkraut are always served in very generous portions. As long as the squadron is not actually at sea, the troops receive meat and soup from time to time. A great open kettle is used to cook for all the non-commissioned officers, soldiers, and sailors, whose number

Aboard a Dutch Troop Transport
en route to South Africa, 1802

consists of about 640 persons. When it is meal time, the signal is given by ringing a bell which hangs on the forward part of the ship, whereupon one man from each mess proceeds to the kitchen with a two-handled tub to get the groats, peas, or whatever for his mess. Such a tub is called a "Beck" in the Dutch sailors' slang. [Probably Back and Beck are the same word and the manuscript copyist misread an e for an a in this latter use.] The group which shares eating therefrom is also called a "Beck" or mess, and all such, who belong to one mess or another, are generally referred to as mess folks, to differentiate them from those who eat in cabins. Sundays, Tuesdays, and Thursdays everyone, from non-commissioned officers and upwards, receives a glass of brandy toward noon, and as the ships' captains have joined together, a measured portion of beer is issued daily, also, until the time when the ships clear the channel. Then only brandy will be issued because beer requires too much space. Finally, two large vats filled with water stand on the

Aboard a Dutch Troop Transport
en route to South Africa, 1802

deck, from which, with the use of a tin ladle that is attached, everyone may take and drink as much as he desires, but may not take water away. The government pays the captain of a ship for the food of the mentioned type, at a daily rate of four guilders for staff officers, one guilder and eighteen stoecker for a captain or a subaltern, and eight stoecker for a non-commissioned officer or private.

Several days after the battalion was embarked, everyone from non-commissioned officers upward received, as a gift from the government, a pair of long trousers, and a jacket with sleeves made of blue jersey. Also, along with this gift, there was a leather cap. The uniforms and hats were at once packed in crates brought with us. Cartridge pouches were also packed in cases, but the rifles and muskets, except those needed for daily duty, were stored in the officers' cabins and in the passageways and under the decks, in racks made for that purpose. The troops were allowed to keep their sabers. All military duties, otherwise performed

Aboard a Dutch Troop Transport
en route to South Africa, 1802

by the marines, were now performed by the land forces, and the marines were primarily employed as sailors.

Aboard a Dutch Troop Transport
en route to South Africa, 1802

3

As the ships have only half of their normal complement, and in order to provide some healthy activity for the soldiers during such a long sea voyage, the jaegers and fusiliers performed sailor duties, under the supervision of the non-commissioned officers and corporals, as long as such duty was on deck and not in the rigging. One-half of the battalion had to be on duty at all times, while the other half rested.

16 July - The promotion of Lieutenant Colonel von Wilmowsky to colonel, of Major Mueller to lieutenant colonel, and Captain von Gilten to Major, was announced.

4 August - About six o'clock in the evening a favorable wind, which had been desired for so long a time, finally arose. Although it was so weak that it could hardly be noticed, the commodore gave the signal to raise the first anchor. The squadron then rested on the second anchor, at half an anchor cable length, waiting for the morning flood tide. The

Aboard a Dutch Troop Transport
en route to South Africa, 1802

passage which leads to the sea from this anchorage is so narrow that it can be used by ships of the line only when the wind is from four points, namely, east by southeast, 10, 10 by east, and southeast [sic - no fourth point is listed], and otherwise they must wait for a flood tide, as they have too little water. Smaller ships can exit with other winds, but it is common even for these ships to run aground and to be wrecked during storms. In former times, ships of the line could exit also with sixteen winds, between north and south, but for some years now a new channel has been developing, closer to the island of Texel, which apparently, already in the coming year, will be navigable and will have been marked.

The transport fleet bound for the West Indies, under the command of the sea captain Blos van Treslang, raised anchor and is holding itself ready to get under sail in the morning.

The continuous calm, an absolutely clear sky, the most beautiful sunset, and an increased gaiety because of the music from all the

Aboard a Dutch Troop Transport
en route to South Africa, 1802

warships about to set sail, and all this combined, with the thoughts of the approaching departure from our native soil, and the beginning of a long sea voyage to a distant part of the world, produced within the not-feelingless souls a painfully pleasant sensation.

<u>5 August</u> - At five o'clock in the morning the wind was constantly favorable and strong enough to enable our departure against the flood tide. Therefore the signal was given to take in the second anchor and at eight o'clock the squadron got under sail. The *Bato* was ordered to lead the way, followed by the *Pluto*, the *Kartmaar*, and the *Maria Reigersbergen* brought up the rear while the commandant of the roadstead wished the commodore a good voyage with a thirteen gun salute, to which the latter replied with eleven guns.

The previously mentioned channel, which had caused the delay for the ships of the line, ran alongside the mainland and, at a distance of about fifty paces, passed under the battery from the revolution. Near this battery there is a place

Aboard a Dutch Troop Transport
en route to South Africa, 1802

which is only four and one-half times wider than a ship of the line and which, at flood tide, has a dept of only 26 feet. This spot is known as the "dry hole" [Droogte] and to pass it one of the four named winds, which hold the ships away from the land, is necessary. At the same time the rudder is held toward the land, and in this manner, by means of the two opposing forces, the desired course is steered.

It is easy to understand the joy which swept the *Bato* and the *Pluto* when they had passed the "dry hole" by twelve o'clock. The *Kartmaar* was not fortunate enough to share this joy, because at this place, it ran aground. The *Maria Reigersbergen*, on the other hand, being a frigate, did not need as much depth of water, passed through the channel and followed without having to stop. Still, it must be noted, that the three ships of the line, each of which draws 24 feet, make it understandable how much caution must be used to pass a place where the water is only 26 feet. Above all, it was fortunate that the difficulty occurred with

Aboard a Dutch Troop Transport
en route to South Africa, 1802

the last and not with the middle ship, because otherwise the first ship would have had to turn back until the last one was able to make its exit.

Toward one o'clock, except for the Kartmaar, which had run aground and was now left to its fate, the squadron was outside the harbor and the commodore was welcomed into the sea by the entrance fort, as well as by the commander of the West Indies fleet, with a thirteen guns salute from each. The first was thanked with the same number and the latter with eleven shots. Here the pilots left the ships, which they had guided from the roadstead into the sea, and also lost the authority which they had had during that time, because even the commodore, as long as the pilots were on board, had no authority concerning the management of his own ship, but the latter were in complete command. On the other hand, they were also held responsible for any accident, resulting from their directions.

While our squadron and the West Indian transport fleet were departing, the coast was

Aboard a Dutch Troop Transport
en route to South Africa, 1802

lined with people, part who came from Holland to wish their relatives and friends a last farewell, part from the nearby coastal villages, who hastened here so as not to miss the chance to see the splendid sight, not seen for many years, of more than thirty ships, a result of the present peace and prospects of seeing a new development of trade, whose inactivity had been depressing. The scene was peaceful and beautiful. Parents, children, brothers, sisters, wives, and other relatives, friends, both male and female, waved to wish good fortune as long as individuals were recognizable, with handkerchiefs, and then used them in turn, due to the pain of parting, to dry the tears they could not hold back.

The wind grew stronger and toward seven o'clock the Holland coast was lost from view. Farewell dear ones, who have treated me so motherly, sisterly, congenially, and friendly. I have an inner feeling of appreciation for the countless proofs of your love. My profession now tears me from your embrace, and sends me

Aboard a Dutch Troop Transport
en route to South Africa, 1802

more than one thousand miles from you. I would do you an injustice if I needed to request that, in spite of the distance, I should not be lost from your memory. Your faces, no matter where I may be, will remain constantly among my most vivid memories. In my mind I will be seated with you and talk with you as if in your presence, and in this manner, in this fantasy, partially compensate for the actual loss. Should the guiding destiny of the great, human fate decree the greatest good fortune, which I can imagine, still dearest mother, beloved brothers and sisters, and relatives, the cherished friends, I will again find, with every reminiscence, after the passage of time, valued and longed-for situation. What indescribable joy I already anticipate at this fortunate time. Nothing, no matter what it might be, can be of such worth to me, that I would trade our reunion, recount our experiences while separated from one another, and bask in our glorious lives.

6 August - The wind was very strong and absolutely unfavorable. Therefore the squadron

Aboard a Dutch Troop Transport
en route to South Africa, 1802

found it necessary to cruise between the A-bank and the Galloper Bank. The usual seasickness rather generally set in.

For the Holland mariners the following listed divisions of time are used, and the time is measured by the use of an hour-glass. When the hour-glass is empty, half an hour has passed, and this measure of time is called a glass. This is brought to everyone's attention by a stroke on the bell hanging on the forward part of the ship. The emptying of the second glass is made known by two strokes of the bell, and so it continues through eight glasses, which then receives the name of the watch. Six of these watches constitute 24 hours, and are called a meal [Essmal or Satmal]. The individual watches have the following names:

Evenings from 8 to 12 o'clock - first watch
Evenings from 12 to 4 o'clock - dog watch
From 4 to 8 o'clock - day watch
From 12 to 4 o'clock - morning watch
From 4 to 8 o'clock - dog watch

[It is clear that some confusion exists in the

Aboard a Dutch Troop Transport
en route to South Africa, 1802

above list of watches, both as to times and designations.] As soon as a ship enters the ocean, duty is started according to the watch schedule. The three senior officers, or those who are the most capable, arrange among themselves, and each takes such a four hour watch, during which time he is responsible for the management and supervision of the watch. The remaining officers are divided among those three officers. Likewise, the three senior helmsmen arrange their watches among themselves. The sailors are divided into two equal parts, of which the first, during the noted watch, must be prepared for all work, while the other lies in their hammocks, and it continues in this manner, until a situation arises which threatens the ship. Then everyone, without exception, must be at his assigned post. There is no difference made in this duty system by day or night. Whoever is not on duty, goes to bed without worrying whether it is midday or midnight, and, according to the system, this is really necessary.

Aboard a Dutch Troop Transport
en route to South Africa, 1802

The jaegers and fusiliers of the battalion are, as already mentioned, likewise divided into two sections, which, beginning today, are relieved on watch like the sailors, and under the supervision of their assigned non-commissioned officers perform the work of the sailors insofar as it is not connected with climbing the masts. Also, the subalterns are on duty daily. They are also relieved alternately and have the overall supervision of maintenance of discipline. The military duty is performed daily by a non-commissioned officer, a corporal, a drummer, and eighteen privates, who are under the command of the two designated officers, and relieved with them at eight o'clock in the morning. This watch is armed only with sabers because the movement of the ship on the ocean makes the use of muskets inconvenient, and at the same time dangerous.

Commencing today, everyone received his measured out portion of water, for which purpose, the battalion was issued tin canteens.

Aboard a Dutch Troop Transport
en route to South Africa, 1802

Everyone, regardless of rank, the lieutenant colonel, as well as a private, receives daily not quite a half quart of water, which is given out at eight o'clock in the morning. Anyone who wants to drink tea or coffee must give back to the cook an equal amount from his issued water, for which reason the officers take only half of their ration and receive the rest each morning as hot water.

Aboard a Dutch Troop Transport *en route* to South Africa, 1802

4

<u>7 August</u> - The wind continued constantly favorable. About five o'clock in the morning our ship had 32 fathoms of water, and suddenly only eighteen fathoms. At the same time, the throwing lead was covered with stones and shells from which it was determined that we were in the vicinity of a bank. The commodore gave the order, with a signal, for the squadron to turn. It was determined that we were only eight ship lengths from the Galloper Bank, and we were very happy to have been so fortunate as to avoid this danger.

<u>8 August</u> - During the morning thick fog and continued unfavorable wind. During the previous night, the *Bato* and the *Maria Reigersbergen* had become separated from us. In order to avoid an accident between the banks, we returned to the depth of the Meuse River. From about noon until evening, the West Indian transport fleet of 23 sail was in sight, and also had to cruise about.

<u>9 August</u> - The wind was more favorable,

Aboard a Dutch Troop Transport
en route to South Africa, 1802

although it was very weak and variable. The course was again set toward the English Channel. About nine o'clock in the morning the *Bato* was to be seen and by evening had returned to us. Toward six o'clock in the evening the English, and soon thereafter, the French coasts were visible. At nine-thirty the first lighthouse was seen, which our seamen had so impatiently looked for.

10 August - At two o'clock in the morning a full calm developed and at the same time, a very strong current flowed toward the English coast, so that we dropped anchor and gave the *Bato* the signal to do the same. Toward noon an officer was sent out in a boat to determine the depth of water at various distances. An exceptionally large number of brown fish were seen. As the wind picked up somewhat, both ships raised anchor at two-thirty in the afternoon and by six-thirty in the evening, the castle at Dover and the roadstead of Duyas were to be seen. However, because of contrary winds and strong currents, we dropped anchor

Aboard a Dutch Troop Transport
en route to South Africa, 1802

at seven-thirty, about four miles from the coast.

<u>11 August</u> - In the morning, about two o'clock, a very strong and completely adverse wind arose, and because the ships were in great danger between the reefs present here, the anchor was quickly raised again, and we sailed eight miles out into the ocean. The *Bato* was aware that it was very near the Falstar Reef, and therefore, felt compelled to cut the anchor cable, fearing that the strong winds would drive it against the mentioned reef. Such an anchor cable costs the Republic about two thousand guilders, and here this was lost in just a moment. At five o'clock in the morning the West Indian transport fleet was again in sight, and then again disappeared. During the afternoon the strength of the wind decreased, but remained unfavorable. Toward six o'clock in the evening, three Dutch ships of the line, *Brutus, Neptune,* and *Van de Witt,* and the brig *Ajax,* under the command of Vice Admiral Horzing, approached. This squadron had sailed to Santo Domingo in December with French

Aboard a Dutch Troop Transport
en route to South Africa, 1802

troops, and was now on its return voyage. Boats with officers from the admiral's ship and the *Ajax*, which passed closest to us, came on board our ship to inquire about news from the fatherland. The commodore gave each of them about two pecks of fresh potatoes, which were a very fine and welcome gift after a long period without fresh vegetables. The sailors of the admiral's ship, as well as those of the *Ajax* gave three cheers as they sailed past, which each time, including the last, was answered by the sailing master with a signal on his pipe. The sailing master is the senior non-commissioned officer in precedence, and is responsible for maintaining the weapons, sails, lines, etc., in good order. Carpenters, sail makers, and canvas sewers, as well as all seamen necessary for the work details, are under his orders, and he is expected to have special abilities. Below him are the boatswain, and the boatswain's mate, the former having responsibility for the mainmast, the latter for the foremast, and all that pertains to them, including supervision

Aboard a Dutch Troop Transport
en route to South Africa, 1802

over the seamen assigned to work there. The mizzenmast with its rigging is under the supervision of the senior quartermaster on ships of the line. The remaining petty officers are divided among other positions of lesser responsibility. Likewise, all the seamen are divided, part for instance having all the work and maintenance of the mizzensails, another handles the foresails and is called the foresails company, and so everyone aboard a warship has his assigned post, which eliminates all confusion, and over all, the sailing master has responsibility.

Confusion would result if everyone who was responsible for supervision of various tasks called out to his subordinates instructions concerning their work during strong wind gusts or in battle, when no one would be able to hear the sailing master, the boatswain, the boatswain's mate, the quartermaster, in short, any petty officer. Therefore, each is provided with a silver or copper pipe, which has an exceptionally clear and penetrating tone, and by

Aboard a Dutch Troop Transport
en route to South Africa, 1802

means of a hole can produce a surprising number of sounds. The commanding officer, during a maneuver which the ship must execute, makes his orders known with the help of a megaphone, and the petty officers then use the mentioned pipes to give known signals to their subordinates as to the necessary tasks to perform. As an example, if sixty or more men, during the handling of a sail, should pull on a line, this takes place with a certain signal for each heave, whereby the strength is fully concentrated and even in this task the pipe serves a purpose.

12 August - Because of continued contrary winds, constant tacking. Therefore, the West Indian transport fleet was in sight all day.

13 August - After midnight the wind became completely favorable, which allowed us to profit from it. In the morning, at six-thirty, I discovered the English, and shortly thereafter, the French coasts. About ten o'clock we were opposite Duyas, at a distance of two miles, and saw the *Maria Reigersbergen* lying at anchor in

Aboard a Dutch Troop Transport
en route to South Africa, 1802

the roadstead there, having sailed there to wait our arrival after having separated from us during the night of the seventh to the eighth. The commodore made signal for her to get under sail, and to follow us, which she understood and acknowledged, and at four o'clock in the afternoon, she joined us. The weather was exceptionally fine, and the churches and houses in Calais were clearly visible through the telescope. We passed so near the English coast, between Duyas and Dover, that, even without a telescope, people could be seen moving on the shore. About two o'clock in the afternoon we were near Dover, where we lay to, in order to let an English pilot, who had come aboard during the morning to offer his services, to return to shore, and to await delivery aboard ship of fresh meat, vegetables, beer, and bread, ordered from Dover. In addition, this was such an ideal place to lay to in calm weather, because it was possible for the ship to remain in place without dropping an anchor. Several of my comrades

Aboard a Dutch Troop Transport
en route to South Africa, 1802

and I allowed ourselves, among others, to bring beer to the ship, for which we would have had to pay twelve and one-half guilder per keg, delivered, but were fortunate enough to be put ashore.

The English coast here presents a pleasant view and the surprise is all the greater, when one comes here from the monotonous, sandy, and barren coast of Holland, where only rabbits are present, and each year thousands are spent in order to retain at least the sand dunes so that the ocean does not leave its bounds.

Cliffs of chalk rising straight up are the basis, part joined, part divided by the ravines separating hills, whose varying heights form the coast, which presents a very picturesque view. On the hills, orchards are to be seen, grazing cattle, and flocks of sheep, horses, and the native farmers engaged in tending their fields. Dover lies directly on the ocean, and on both sides hills rise, whose height differentiates them from the cliffs. Seen from the sea, there is a castle on the hill to the right, which is fortified

Aboard a Dutch Troop Transport
en route to South Africa, 1802

in the ancient manner, with walls and towers. Lower down, however, it has been strengthened with newer construction. Beyond the city lies a large and splendid valley, which gives a pleasant view of orchards and fields of grain. Also, in this valley, all sorts of livestock were to be seen, proof of the fertility of the coastal region. At a great distance inland this valley is again closed in by high hills on which orchards, trees, and brushwood create a changing scenery between Duyas and Dover. This provides a striking impression, especially when one catches sight of a manor in a distant glen. The view of this beautiful coast line, today's clear, bright sky, and the joy to be finally off the odious North Sea and within the English Channel, in general created high spirits among us.--- Toward four o'clock in the afternoon, the squadron got under way again and gradually withdrew from the land about six o'clock, so that with twilight it had nearly disappeared from sight.

Aboard a Dutch Troop Transport *en route* to South Africa, 1802

5

<u>14 August</u> - About four o'clock in the afternoon we arrived opposite the Isle of Wight, which is also very high and has many hills. We again lay to in order to wait for *Bato,* which fell behind again. At six-thirty it again caught up with us, and because it sails poorly, the commodore decided to leave it behind and to continue onward alone with the *Maria Reigersbergen,* which, after saying farewells through the megaphone, actually happened.

<u>15 August</u> - Early this morning the *Bato* was already out of sight. At five-thirty in the evening we found ourselves near Gouds-Staart, a region of the English coast where an obviously noticeable cape shows opposite, and it will be the last view that we will have of the coast.

<u>16 August</u> - During the afternoon we encountered two English warships, each of fifty guns. In the Channel, and especially at the entrance between Calais and Dover, we found an abundance of sailing ships of every variety.

Aboard a Dutch Troop Transport
en route to South Africa, 1802

<u>17 August</u> - After we had passed through the 96 mile long Channel, this morning we arrived in the Bay of Biscay. Toward midday, a shark was seen near the ship, and after an hour it was caught on a large hook. It was more than six feet five inches long. The skin was comparable in color and appearance to that of an eel, and the streak behind the head was arrow-shaped. The head was about a foot long, and toward the back of the head, about nine inches wide, which gradually narrowed to a rounding off of about an inch and one-half. Underneath the head is quite flat, and above gently arched. The jaws are in the bottom of the head, seven and one-half inches behind the snout, and form a gap of eleven and one-half inches. The second jaw formed a curve toward the front, at the greatest distance from the first of two and one-half inches. This curve forms the opening part of the jaws. The measurements given here are valid only when the jaws are closed, because they are capable of an exceptionally wide expansion. The upper

Aboard a Dutch Troop Transport
en route to South Africa, 1802

and lower jaws were filled with teeth; the lower being one and one-half Linien [a Linien is one-tenth or one-twelfth of an inch] thick; four Linien long, and needle sharp. They are arranged irregularly and so far apart that those in one jaw fit between those of the other jaw. On the head the eyes are eight inches from the tip of the snout, and are about seven Linien in diameter and two and one-half inches apart. The nasal openings contain many folds, and closed, are about four Linien long and three Linien wide. They are located on the lower side of the head, three inches behind the snout. Finally, these sharks, except for the tail fins, which are not like those of the pike and similar fish, but set at an angle, have three fins of which two are one foot long, and at the base are two and one-half inches wide, running to a point located about the middle of the back, but slightly more toward the head, about as long as the others, and three inches at the base. The strength with which the shark, after being pulled aboard, beat about with his tail, was

Aboard a Dutch Troop Transport
en route to South Africa, 1802

exceptional.

During the afternoon a school of more than one hundred brown fish, which came from the west, passed our ship, from which the sailors determined that a strong wind was expected from that direction.

<u>18 August</u> - The wind, which previously was rather weak, began to freshen, and about one o'clock during the night, became westerly, and at the same time, very violent, causing many to become seasick. Today, for the first time, we received stale water, which certainly is not a cure for seasickness. Toward midnight the violence of the wind decreased.

<u>25 August</u> - Since the eighteenth the winds have been variable and nearly constantly unfavorable. Their violence, high seas, and complete calms have alternated. We advanced three miles in 24 hours. When a violent storm ends, 24 or more hours frequently pass and the winds become completely calm, before the seas settle. They roll on, creating high mountains and deep valleys which the sailors call cavern

Aboard a Dutch Troop Transport
en route to South Africa, 1802

seas [Hohle See], and which caused the ship great damage when they collide. Such waves can make a cavern sea very dangerous if the ship is not well constructed. When there is no noticeable wind or one that can barely be detected, because it only has strength enough to raise a few feathers on a very thin thread, it is said to be calm. Then the ship rolls from side to side, and this causes the unpleasant creaking of the masts and other parts of the rigging when it is in such a situation. Toward noon, we passed more than a thousand fish, about three feet long, which among the Dutch seamen are known as porpoise. Their head ends with a snout and is about eight inches long. Fifteen or twenty, or fewer, advance with an unbelievable speed to the right and left of the ship, and give the appearance of being hunted and greatly disturbed. In a rough sea, and when the fish cut through the water vigorously, waves are created ahead of them, which frequently wash high over them on both sides. These waves are called breakers. Breakers also rise when the

Aboard a Dutch Troop Transport
en route to South Africa, 1802

wind violently drives the sea against a coast or when the tide rises.

<u>27 August</u> - During the morning, something was seen floating in the distance which could not be identified through the telescope. Therefore the commodore set out a boat and sent it to investigate. Those sent out discovered it to be a large wooden beam, completely covered with shell fish and with many fish gathered about. One of the latter was caught and brought on board. This one belonged to the kind of fish which does not swim on edge in the water, but on the first side, as for example the flounder, plaice, or similar ones which are generally called flat fish. His length was about three feet and the greatest width was two and one-half feet. In the middle he was eight inches thick. In other respects, however, nearly the figure of a whale, and except for the head, all around rather sharply pointed. The upper side was of a silver-gray color and glistened, and the under side completely white. The skin was sharp and

Aboard a Dutch Troop Transport
en route to South Africa, 1802

well-polished. He had no fish bones, and the outer skin which covered it, could only be cut through with difficulty. On one part of this cartilage there was a very fibrous and fatty flesh, which, however, I believe would make a nourishing and delicious soup. The mouth was exactly like that of a carp, and measured only one inch in diameter. Covering the mouth was a growth which was quite similar to a flattened human nose. The fish was without a tail, in which place was to be found a half-moon shaped notch. On both sides, eight inches from the mentioned growth, fins were visible in the shape of a large oyster shell, and above, as well as below, about the middle of the head, with the uppermost in a crosswise position, one foot long and at the base, four inches wide, and forming a right triangle whose hypotenuse was turned toward the front, were others. The liver was straw-yellow and as large as an average calf's liver. This fish was only recognized by the boatswain and called an "Auld Wyf or old wife, and actually the cut of the mouth, the

Aboard a Dutch Troop Transport
en route to South Africa, 1802

growth resembling a nose, and the position of the eyes gave it a striking resemblance to the haggard and sunken face of an old woman.

<u>28 August</u> - The wind was constantly favorable and strong, so that we covered ten miles in a week [sic]. We were in the latitude of Cape Finisterre and only about thirty miles from it. During the afternoon the wind died completely.

<u>29 August</u> - A French merchant ship which had left Texel on the ninth, overtook us. It was bound for Marseille. From it we received the news that the *Kartmaar*, although undamaged, had returned to the roadstead of Texel and on the ninth was still lying there.

<u>30 August</u> - Sunset this evening was especially beautiful. As the sun nearly touched the horizon, we saw, between us and the sea, at a great distance, but in a direct line, a ship, so that it appeared that a ship with masts and sails actually stood in the sun. This was a pleasing and certainly a seldom encountered view.

<u>3 September</u> - At one o'clock in the

Aboard a Dutch Troop Transport
en route to South Africa, 1802

morning we were in the latitude of the so-called Barlings, in French, les Balenguens, and at a distance from them of about three miles. These Barlings are about four miles from the cliffs of Portugal, three of which, because of their height are especially noticeable. Two of them are long. However, the third is shaped like a pyramid and of the most pronounced height. Many seamen have met their death here during storms, among others, the senior helmsman of our ship was pointedly reminded by the sight of these cliffs of the death of his brother, who had gone down with his ship at this place some years previously. It is customary on all English, Holland, French, and other ships, as soon as they have passed the Barlings, to celebrate, and this occurred on our ship this evening, also. All officers and petty officers and everyone who held any special position, which gave him more income than that of the sailors, the ship's cook being no exception, gathered on the quarterdeck. The sailors assembled on the upper main deck and in the passageways. The

Aboard a Dutch Troop Transport
en route to South Africa, 1802

commodore assured them that all sailors, at this latitude, were obligated by custom, to experience baptism, or to be exempted from this by the payment of one hundred guilder. The baptism consisted of an individual being fastened on a line, then thrown overboard, and dunked in the ocean three times. In general the example of the commodore was followed and each agreed to pay a ransom fee according to his rank and position, which was noted by the ship's scribe. After this was finished, sailors hidden in the crow's nest dumped loads of water, which had been carried up earlier and in secret, so that all those who had not expected it, received a thorough soaking, and this ended the ceremony with those who had been hit with the water being laughed at by the others. The money raised in this manner will be used to buy wine at the Canary Islands, where the ships will halt to take on water, with a certain portion of the wine being issued daily to the sailors passing in the vicinity of the Equator, to serve as nourishment. ---- Because the wind, for some

Aboard a Dutch Troop Transport
en route to South Africa, 1802

days was variable and unfavorable, the commodore decided to sail to Lisbon, and to take on water and other necessities there, with the hope that during that time the wind might change to our advantage. During the evening, about seven o'clock, a Portuguese pilot approached. He was called on board and made an agreement with the commodore to guide us to Lisbon.

4 September - Toward one o'clock in the afternoon, the Portuguese coast came into view, as the continuously unfavorable wind allowed us to proceed only a short distance until we arrived in the latitude of the Tagus River, and then, after turning toward the Tagus, the wind, which had previously been unfavorable, served us somewhat better.

5 September - During the morning, fog and rain prevented us from seeing the coast, but toward noon the weather brightened and became very nice, allowing a surprisingly advantageous view of the majesty of the coast. As far as it can be seen from here, it consists of

Aboard a Dutch Troop Transport
en route to South Africa, 1802

exceptionally high mountains, which form a half-moon and from whose middle the Tagus flows into the ocean. The left end of the half-moon shows an exceptionally high, nearly cliff-like, and, at least on this side, an obviously wild and barren mountain, which has the name St. Roc. It shows a lot of the most beautiful peaks in many forms. On the northern slope of this mountain, a castle is to be seen, in the middle, a nunnery, and on the southern end, a monastery; the latter standing on a remarkably beautiful and high, rocky peak.

Aboard a Dutch Troop Transport
en route to South Africa, 1802

6

After entering the Tagus, whose left bank is completely flat until two miles from Lisbon, a new mountain chain commences and increases as it passes the city. On every level plain, and especially there, where this mountain chain commences, lies a small town, occupied by fishermen. The mountain chain consists of high, rounded, and among themselves, very similar mountains, which are separated from one another by ravines with either gradual or rising slopes. Through the first, the eye can occasionally catch a glimpse of the other mountains in the distance. Vineyards and the homes of the vintners give the mountains an uncommonly pleasant appearance, with their crests being crowned with olive trees. On the right bank of the Tagus, a caldron-shaped valley of many miles in circumference is initially to be seen, formed by the gently sloping mountains which rise near the river. In the valley, country manors with gardens, chapels, and windmills, in an abundance, stand

Aboard a Dutch Troop Transport
en route to South Africa, 1802

in a blending which pleases the eyes. Then a mountain runs along the river which forms a part of every valley, from alternating heights, with first gently, then sharply rising slopes, and hereon Lisbon itself is built. The distances from the mouth of the Tagus to Lisbon is about four miles. About a mile from the mouth, lying on the left bank, is a fort which protects the entrance and serves as a prison for war captives during peacetime. The right bank of the Tagus has an abundance of forts and open batteries which are occupied by an unimaginably large number of troops. The main fort is called Belem, or Bethlehem, and is about three-fourths of a mile from the city. Above this, situated on and beside the previously mentioned mountain, a suburb of Lisbon is visible, which has a scattering of large and small buildings, which like all buildings in this region are white and make a beautiful scene, especially when viewed from a distance. This suburb is connected to Lisbon, itself. The number of windmills which are in the area is

Aboard a Dutch Troop Transport
en route to South Africa, 1802

unbelievable and stirring, in that the arms, without exception, have the form of the cross of St. Andrew.

About four o'clock in the afternoon we lay at anchor opposite the fort of Belem, saluted it with thirteen shots, and then received the same number as a thank you, in return. Then the commodore sent an officer there to request an examination at the earliest time, which service is rendered to all inbound ships to determine if there is any contagious disease on board, as the commodore wished to drop anchor closer to the city, yet today. Shortly thereafter, a medical team of four persons came alongside our ship, whereupon the entire ship's personnel had to show themselves in the passageways and on deck, and the commodore gave the team a written assurance that there was no contagious disease on board. Then this ceremony was ended, but repeated aboard the *Maria Reigersbergen*. Then the anchor was again raised, we sailed further up the river, and half a mile below Lisbon, lay to with two anchors.

Aboard a Dutch Troop Transport
en route to South Africa, 1802

<u>6 September</u> - In the morning the ship's personnel were told of an old Portuguese law, which forbade anyone to sell or trade tobacco with the Portuguese, on penalty of a 200,000 Reis punishment. As the German dollar [Reichsthaler] is unknown in Portugal, and one generally figures in Reis, an uncommon coin, which has a value of a Holland penny, therefore the punishment, as I estimate according to the original law, of such an amount of Reis, when converted to German dollars, means 200,000 Reis amount to 632 and one-half Holland guilder, and how many strangers come to Portugal who can pay this 200,000 Reichsthaler [sic - Reis?] punishment? The mentioned law also forbids those going on land, from the ships, to carry pointed knives, scissors, and such instruments.

During the time we were lying before Lisbon, I often went into the city, and gathered, in so far as the opportunity arose, information about the city.

Lisbon belongs among the great cities of the

Aboard a Dutch Troop Transport
en route to South Africa, 1802

second rank. A number of splendid public, as well as private buildings, are to be seen, although not all buildings present a pleasing appearance. Also, the maintenance of their exteriors appear to receive little attention, and even, on the other hand, the eye is often insulted by the deterioration of the coloring of the walls and the contrasting color of the windows, door, and such. In general, the buildings are covered with white plaster, or only occasionally painted yellow. The roofs are covered with a double layer of tile, of which the lower covering is laid in the usual manner. Each tile of the upper covering however, is fitted so that two of the lower ones have their joint covered. Furthermore, they are then joined together with quicklime, so that from the back of each tile of the upper covering, only about a width of two inches is to be seen. Because the city, as already indicated earlier, lies on a high mountain, the streets which lead to it are so steep that it is not without danger that vehicles use them. Supposedly during

Aboard a Dutch Troop Transport
en route to South Africa, 1802

violent and persistent rainy weather, the water rushes down these streets with a depth of one foot. The pavement is almost always good and well maintained, and it is composed of exceptionally hard blue stones. From the roadstead, the city presents a magnificent view. It rises, much as daybreak, because the buildings lower down are for the most part small houses [Palhaeuser], which are set off by the stately, high mountains, and high above these lies a sort of citadel on a beautiful peak. This citadel is reached on foot only with a noticeable effort, but then one is rewarded by a wonderful view. Three recently built streets in the level area in the upper city differentiate themselves from the rest of the city by their regularity. Their names are the Silver, Gold, and Fabric Streets. The buildings on these streets are each and everyone of the same size, fifty paces long and four stories high. Every two such buildings are separated from the others by a narrow cross street. The three main streets are fourteen paces wide and in addition,

Aboard a Dutch Troop Transport
en route to South Africa, 1802

provided with a foot path three paces wide, and paved with square blocks of stone, which are separated from the streets by a row of posts [Polarin], two feet thick and four paces from one another.

No true Waldecker would visit Lisbon without visiting the grave of Prince Christian of Waldeck. Lieutenant Colonel Mueller, Major von Gilten, Lieutenant Stoecker, my brother, and I joined together on the pilgrimage and were escorted by the Danish Ambassador to Portugal, Chamberlain von Warnstaedt, who appeared to respect the memorial to our beloved prince. We found the grave in the cemetery, lying immediately beyond the English hospital. It has a narrow configuration and has a lane bordered with tall cypress trees leading through it. Toward the end of this lane, on the right hand side, the monument is to be seen, because of its height. It is surrounded by many others, mostly of English, and also by cypress trees. Here the prince rests. The stone is of alabaster, which has been cut for this

Aboard a Dutch Troop Transport
en route to South Africa, 1802

monument, and is a four-sided pyramid on whose right and left sides small urns have been cut. On the upper front side the strikingly life-like bust of the prince stands in relief within a laurel wreath, on metal. Beneath this is the following inscription:

Christiano Augusto
Caroli Augusti Frederici
Principis Waldecii Filio
Qui visit an LIIII
Deces. VIII kal. Oktobr. DDDCCLXXXVIII
Johannes
Lusitannae Princeps Regius
Qui ut vixi Rex Militaris Peritissimi
Opera Uteratur
Enn a Germania vocaverat
Hoc Mommentum
P.C.

Under this inscription is a crossed dagger and a torch, bound together with a laurel wreath. Finally, beneath this is a helmet, held

Aboard a Dutch Troop Transport
en route to South Africa, 1802

on each side by a Fama [?], which final symbol rests on a bough. Also, the house in which the prince resided until his death, is one of interest to Waldeckers. It is large, has a fine appearance from without, and stands in the Ruade St, Francisco de Bovia Street.

Among the unbelievable large number of churches, especially noteworthy are Loracode Jesus "Heart of Jesus" and St. Roos. The first was built by the present queen, because of the following event. She was threatened with death because of consumption. All the medical efforts tried were unsuccessful, and finally a cure was decided upon which was already well-known in ancient times, and which had provided hope of a cure when recommended by the famous Dutch doctor, Boorhafen. The queen therefore was advised to sleep beside a healthy person in order to seek a cure by inhaling that person's breath. However, the choice of such a person was not an easy one. Poor girls from among the population would have been easy to find, who would have risked

Aboard a Dutch Troop Transport
en route to South Africa, 1802

losing their health for an adequate payment. But, how could the Queen of Portugal, despite the fact that her life depended upon it, so forget her position as to allow such a person to sleep in her bed? This was certainly not acceptable, but the selected person must naturally be a member of the oldest nobility. A long search among those families was made, but no young girl would offer to assume such a dangerous honor. Finally, a young girl was found, who decided to risk her life for the queen, and she possessed the proper credentials and was a member of one of the oldest families. The queen regained her health, built a nunnery, and designated the aforesaid girl to be the abbess. The mentioned church, however, belonged to the order of Lozacao de Jesus. It had the configuration of a cross on whose lower end of the east entrance was to be found, opposite the upper end of the choir and in the main altar, as well as on both ends of the cross, which passed before the choir, two small altars. The length of the church up to the choir is sixty paces, that

Aboard a Dutch Troop Transport
en route to South Africa, 1802

beyond, 32 paces, and of the two side arms, in which the small altars are to be found an equal distance. The width of all arms is sixteen paces. The floor is covered with exceptionally smoothly polished slabs of the finest alabaster. The ceiling, a flat surface, appears to be painted in a Greek fashion. The figures are, however, formed from fine colored stone in the German method. Over each of the two altars, outside the choir, a canopy rests on two sixteen feet high columns of jasper. In the long arm hang six, and in those which cut across sideways, four exceptionally large chandeliers over each of the previously noted eight small altars, all similar, all of silver, and very heavy. In addition, all altars, large and small, are provided with more than adequate candlesticks of all sorts and sizes, and of the same metal. Above all, those in the alcoves, especially the three large ones noted, have a boundless lavish splendor. The smallest wooden object to be seen in this church is made of Brazil wood, including the doors and such. In short, no cost

Aboard a Dutch Troop Transport
en route to South Africa, 1802

was spared in the construction and decorations, and the previously mentioned Danish Ambassador assured us that the total sum amounted to fifteen million escudos, which amounts to about 22 and ½ million Dutch guilder. The previously mentioned first abbess of the order is no longer living. In the middle of the church stands a sentry with a weapon held high in his right hand, the head bared, and the helmet in the left hand, In this manner, passing officers are honored.

.

Aboard a Dutch Troop Transport
en route to South Africa, 1802

7

The church of St. Roos is of no consequence in and of itself, but one of the altars therein is definitely worth seeing. This is to be found in one of the remaining parts of the church, in a very well guarded chapel, separated from the church and having iron doors. The unimaginable worth of this altar, is that it is made entirely of silver is not the attraction, but three pieces of mosaic work catch the eye, which can not be torn away without effort. The baptism of Jesus by John in the Jordan, the appearance of the angel Gabriel to Mary, and her conception are presented in this manner. The first is to be seen above the altar and with the two others beside it. Unbelievable is the illusion which exists with these pieces. One believes he sees the finest paintings, but nevertheless, they are set together in an unbelievable artistic manner, with small colored stones of the exact shading of light and shadows. This was first fully demonstrated when the design of the third of these pieces was

Aboard a Dutch Troop Transport
en route to South Africa, 1802

to be seen, when closely examined, following an accident. In addition, there is also a sacristy shown in this church which contains a treasury of gold and silver church vessels, and some biblical tales are portrayed in relief in silver. At the same time, many relics are safeguarded therein, such as the skull of the Holy Benedict and Corlestin, which last is provided with excellent, strong teeth; and thigh bones from the Holy Clement and Donat. All of which are in filigreed, silver chests.---The exchange encloses a part of the Placo de Lombricio, or Trading Square. It is, not including park houses and the connecting corridor, about thirty paces long and equally as wide, and completely covered, with the covering being vaulted and resting on sixteen columns. This well-known square is also known by the designation of King Joseph Square because the statue of the king stands there. This statue is of the king mounted on a horse, and is of colossal size and of cast bronze, with various symbols about it, and faces the Tagus. On the pedestal a warship

Aboard a Dutch Troop Transport
en route to South Africa, 1802

under full sail is shown in relief, in bronze, which makes for excellent viewing.---

The Russian Square which also serves as a parade ground for the garrison, is of regular dimensions and about four hundred paces long and equally as wide. A part is bordered by the stately, large Inquisition Building. --- Not far from this square are the public gardens, enclosed by a brick wall, in which there are window-like openings, seven feet high and five feet wide, from twelve to twelve [sic] paces apart, and four feet above the ground. The openings are closed with iron bars. The gardens themselves have a depth of 450 paces and a width of 100 paces. A lane, eighteen paces wide and lined with silver poplar and three unknown types of trees extends throughout the length, dividing the gardens into two equal parts. Each of these two parts is further divided by six, not as wide lanes, which for the most part consists of laurel trees, many of which are from 36 to 46 feet tall; most of which have a trunk of five inches in diameter,

Aboard a Dutch Troop Transport
en route to South Africa, 1802

with a few being eight inches in diameter. In all of these lanes, high myrtle hedges stand amidst brickwork covered tombs, and the remainder of the grounds of the gardens is covered with stucco blocks.--- Completely on the other side of the city, near the Tagus, lies the vegetable, fruit, and fish market, a square in configuration, which is divided into four equal, smaller sections, by a five paces wide crosswalk. The whole consists of 32 halls covered with rather level tiled roofs, resting on stone columns. Each is twelve paces long and eight paces wide, and each two are divided from the others by a two paces wide passage. At the present season of the year, all sorts of vegetables and fruits are being delivered to the local area, they were to be seen assembled here, and one could not expect to find a more excellent grade of perfection of all these than were produced in the local, fortunate climate. All types of pears, apples, plums, almonds, and nuts are available in an abundance. Sour and sweet citrus fruit, also lemons and melons of

Aboard a Dutch Troop Transport
en route to South Africa, 1802

excellent size and beauty are to be seen. The figs are above criticism and grapes of all sorts have attained an uncommon perfection.

Especially worth seeing is the local aqueduct, through which is directed the water needed by the city, from exceptionally high mountains which lie at a distance of six hours. The water conduit is without pumping machinery and functions solely due to the change in elevation, flowing first over and then under the earth, and over mountains and valleys. The single conduit through which the water is carried is nine feet wide and equally as high. On each side is to be found, beneath the level, a rounded channel made of a sort of white marble, a foot wide and equally as deep. The water only flows in one of these channels and the other serves when the situation arises that repair is needed in the other. Where this conduit runs under ground, it is covered with a vault, and where it is on the surface, it is covered by a roof two feet above it. The bottom is paved with square stones, and it is

Aboard a Dutch Troop Transport
en route to South Africa, 1802

possible, as this description already states, to pass through from Lisbon to the source. At a distance of one hundred paces from one to another, nine high towers stand along the conduit, and these are provided on all sides with a number of openings to bring the necessary fresh air into the conduit, and in this manner especially prevent the spoiling of the water. About an hour from Lisbon the aqueduct crosses over an exceptionally deep abyss. Here the aqueduct is provided on both sides with a five feet wide, uncovered walkway, which at the same time serves pedestrians as a bridge, as otherwise, in order to take advantage of work opportunities, because the mentioned abyss is impossible to pass through, they would have to make a long detour. These walkways are paved with square stones, and have a railing made of the same, a foot thick. The entire structure being carried on 36 arches, the height makes a person weak-kneed when he looks down over the middle of the abyss. Further, one can not view this project without wonder. As a proof of

Aboard a Dutch Troop Transport
en route to South Africa, 1802

how well it is constructed, the most severe earthquakes have done it no damage.

One-half hour beyond the mentioned abyss, the village of Beneficy lies in an exceptionally romantic region. Here, as in the area of the village called Alacanta, opposite the city, the most beautiful manor and gardens are to be seen, among which the most outstanding is that of the Marquis de Brandes. Unaccustomed to seeing lemons, oranges, and such, and the related greenhouses, they gave me a great pleasure.

My knowledge of music is limited, but I wish to say something about the local opera, which is, according to strangers who attend the most famous opera, one of the very best. The building is very spacious and the interior tastefully decorated. The decorations and furnishings are in keeping with the purpose, and guarantee the intended illusion in the highest degree. Also, a well developed engineering aspect contributes to the theater. Herr Christian, a eunuch, is the lead singer, and

Aboard a Dutch Troop Transport
en route to South Africa, 1802

Demoiselle Catalana, the leading female singer. The pay of the first, including his extraordinary benefits, supposedly is 20,000 escudo, or about 30,000 Dutch guilders; and of the latter, 30,000 escudo, or 45,000 Dutch guilder. The orchestra is composed of nearly one hundred instruments. The opera receives a subsidy from the king when the recipes are insufficient. I have attended three presentations, and will always have fond memories of the pleasure which I found there. Most notably the solos of Herr Christian and Demoiselle Catalana will never be forgotten. It is surprising how far both have carried their talent and the impression, which they make on their audience, is long-lasting and great. The audience holds its breath when one or both together sing. The ballet dancers' talent is not to be criticized, but neither is it of equal note.

The complexion of the local inhabitants, who find it necessary to be most exposed to the heat of the sun, is a sort of yellow-brown. I have never seen more unpleasant facial features

Aboard a Dutch Troop Transport
en route to South Africa, 1802

of all sorts than here. It is not the features in general, in which the unpleasantness lies, because most can not be said to be unpleasant, but in the display of a certain repulsive, misanthropic and evil characteristic appearance which is noticeable and so frequently encountered.

The dress of the lowest class is very poor and consists of only the most necessary items, but nevertheless, one seldom sees them wearing a sort of smock, or coat, which they carry on their arm, or stock. Also, the women of well-to-do citizens wear cloth coats and certainly this item of clothing in a warm climate, where the cold is an exception, is of doubtful necessity. Nevertheless, it appears to be part of the national costume. Further, both males and females, even the lower classes, in general, carry parasols. The farmer who drives his donkey before him, in addition to his coat, also has a parasol, and I have even seen mules pulling a postillion equipped with such. The farmers' wives wear a sort of cap which appears

Aboard a Dutch Troop Transport
en route to South Africa, 1802

to be made of cardboard covered with cloth of various colors and much of the shape of a fusilier's cap, or a loaf of sugar. The farmers cover their heads with a round hat of such breadth that it extends beyond the shoulders. The upper classes dress in French or English styles.

Horse drawn buggies are seldom seen, but the people use mules instead, which locally, because of the steep, hilly streets, are certainly used to advantage. As a rule, people use a two-wheeled wagon with a two mule team pulling it, of which one is hitched between the shafts and the other, on which the driver sits, runs beside the first. This method of driving is unarguably the safest, because the driver has his animal under complete control, which explains the ease with which the carts are maneuvered in the steep streets. The dress of the drivers and attendants is often very rich, but most achieved without good taste.--- To take things from one place to another, a wagon with two wheels is used which generally is pulled by a span of two

Aboard a Dutch Troop Transport
en route to South Africa, 1802

oxen, usually of great size and strength. These wagons are of a special sort. The wheels of these wagons do not rotate about the wagon's axle as is usual, but are firmly and solidly attached so that the entire axle and wheels turn together under the wagon. The loads which are carried on such wagons, with only a span of two oxen, is unbelievable. The farmers bring their produce to the city on donkeys. Both types of animals, oxen and donkeys, are controlled, not with whips, but the driver is armed with a five foot long pole provided with a pointed end. The drivers are very adept at using these instruments. They walk in the middle of their oxen, and without casting a glance about, without fail, stick one or the other just above the shoulder blade. Mules are ridden, in general, and regardless of social class, and especially when on a journey.

Aboard a Dutch Troop Transport *en route* to South Africa, 1802

8

The stench is the main impression which is encountered upon entering Lisbon, and it is truly of the most unpleasant type, as a frightful odor momentarily overcomes the nose. It is easy to understand the cause, but the eyes can see it one hundred times easier. The filth in the streets is beyond understanding. No one thinks of cleaning the area around his own house or that any other measures should be taken, and therefore, everywhere there is unseemliness, entrails of slaughtered animals, refuse from fruits and vegetables, and such, thrown out of the house and left lying. The contents of very large earthenware vessels is thrown out the window, into the street, in the evening, and at the same time, especially after ten o'clock, it is necessary to walk in the middle of the street to avoid being injured by these vessels, or even killed. That the chamber pots are emptied into the street, goes without saying. What would have seemed unlikely to me, if I had not seen it, is, that even dead donkeys and large and small

Aboard a Dutch Troop Transport
en route to South Africa, 1802

dogs are left lying in the street, to rot. All of this is certainly sufficient to bring out the most unbearable stench, and if the air in this region were not so pure and healthy, there would be frequent visits by pestilent disease.

Therefore, this propensity of the local inhabitants toward boundless uncleanliness gives the dogs, of which many serve as food and therefore disappear, a special value, and they are even under police protection. The number must be very considerable, as there are an estimated four thousand who have no owner and are on their own. Among such a number of dogs, rabies can frequently be expected, and the more so, as they are subject to high heat from the sun, so it comes as no surprise that almost nothing is heard of it. Every resident is bound to set out a dish of water, before his house, for the dogs, every noon, although this precaution is insufficient to prevent the danger.

The organization of the police was more of the kind to protect the lives of inhabitants and strangers and to allow them to enjoy their

Aboard a Dutch Troop Transport
en route to South Africa, 1802

property. In order to guarantee this, and above all, to give the police more strength, the government, about seven months ago, created a so-called police guard, consisting of fifteen hundred men, part dragoons [mounted], part infantry [on foot], who have many responsibilities, to pursue murderers and robbers, and further to have all necessary talents for their posts. For this reason more than once they have already been shot at, but this has not caused them to shrink from their duty. Prior to the establishment of this police guard, many murdered and bound and robbed persons were to be found on the streets every morning. Still, an estimated twenty murders are committed every month in and around Lisbon, although since establishment of the police guard, more than six thousand people have been arrested by them. It is estimated that 4,500 of these have been arrested and not yet tried, of which 1,500 are held in the castle and 3,000 in very large buildings not far therefrom. The scene, which presents itself when one passes these buildings ,

Aboard a Dutch Troop Transport
en route to South Africa, 1802

is horrible. Against every window therein, of which there are a great many, and well protected by iron bars, ten, fifteen, and even more men, mostly with no clothing on their poor body, constantly press, stretching out their arms and begging passers-by for alms. Even the royal servants are not protected from the attacks of robbers. About ten months ago the first chamberlain of the prince-regent, traveling on the road from Lisbon to Caluche, at a distance of two hours from Lisbon and at a suburb of Caluche, was robbed and wounded by a shot in the arm. One coach driver recognized one of the sixteen men of the band, all of them were from the army, and one was beheaded and two were hanged. Now, along this road, there are police guard posts, which are so spaced that they can support one another. In the city proper, murders and robberies are facilitated at night because of the darkness, as the streets are not lighted by lanterns, as would be expected in a place of this size. The Marquis Francisco de Almado, Governor of

Aboard a Dutch Troop Transport
en route to South Africa, 1802

Porto, who is very rich and in general much beloved, presented a plan a few weeks ago for raising a fund for lighting Lisbon, for which purpose he at once offered his personal donation of 30,000 escudo, and it is hoped that this plan will be supported and succeed.--- Concerning the inns, what one finds missing in neatness in the rooms and at meals, without taking note of the unseemliness, is more the scarcity of good furnishings and order, which causes an unfavorable impression. However, there is no complaint about the preparation of the food. The fowls are exceptionally fat and taste good, and apparently many of them are eaten. They are to be had daily, in a variety, at a special market. Unpeeled, but cooked, potatoes are always served. The usual wines are Madeira and port, and other than these, one drinks a mixture of water and ordinary cognac, which does not cost much. The water is especially good, served abundantly in earthenware jars of a special form, instead of cork, and flavored with a fresh lemon. The

Aboard a Dutch Troop Transport
en route to South Africa, 1802

previously mentioned water conduit carries the water into a very large structure containing the primary container, from which the water carriers, who form a guild and are provided with a small brass shield showing their number, deliver it for a fixed price. Generally milk is not brought into the city from the land, but in the morning the farm women milk the quantity each person desires from their cows in the public squares. Another custom which struck me at the inns, which are there, was that dessert was served in distinctive glasses with tooth picks cut out of boxwood.

Prices at the inns are not very cheap. The amount of the check which is presented when the value of the proper coins is known, is truly shocking, because everything is quoted in Reis, as already mentioned above. Breakfast for a group of nine people, in which I found myself, cost 7,000 Reis, or about 22 Dutch guilder. This was in an English inn. In a German inn, I paid 3,540 Reis, or about 11 and ½ Dutch guilder, for me and two guests for a noon meal,

Aboard a Dutch Troop Transport
en route to South Africa, 1802

two bottles of Madeira and an equal amount of port wine, and coffee. Another time I paid 950 Reis, something over 2 and ½ Dutch guilder, for a noon meal for myself alone, and a half bottle of Madeira. As a souvenir, I have attached [missing] both of the first checks, in their original form.

The lowest floor of the houses which stand in the mountains, and which constitute the greatest number in the city, are not inhabited, but in the houses of the most important people, serve as stalls for horses and, more so, for mules. In those of the lower classes, cobblers and other such persons of this type occupy the lowest floor, and donkeys are often seen there, also. The upper floors are completely separated from those beneath by a door and the latter, during the day, appears to be a public shelter for poor persons and donkey drivers. Therefore, it is easily understood, that when entering such a house, it seems unlikely that it is a human residence until the second floor is reached, where the appearance changes

Aboard a Dutch Troop Transport
en route to South Africa, 1802

noticeably. In the lowest floors unseemliness is prevalent, and present to the same degree as in the streets. This overall abundant unseemliness has the disadvantage, that this naturally attracts many flies and mosquitoes, and it is unbelievable in what numbers these annoying insects are to be encountered. Complete sections of the city, especially market places, where cheap food is available, are covered with them, and in stores for copper and lead wares, among others, the color of the wares is difficult to distinguish, as the flies have so fully fouled them.

Aboard a Dutch Troop Transport
en route to South Africa, 1802

9

Truly, I would have liked to have visited a part of the surrounding area, and also regions more distant from Lisbon. In reality, Lieutenant Colonel Mueller and I had agreed to make a journey on mules to the region lying six hours distance, from which the water is carried to Lisbon, and which is supposedly very beautiful and worth seeing. But the indecisiveness of the commodore in determining the length of our stay locally, prevented us from carrying out the proposed plan. Also, it was disappointing for us to forego the opportunity to view the military points of interest, but the time was too short to make the necessary contacts. In my thoughts on leaving Lisbon, I still remember the local gondoliers. The conduct of these people would nowhere be considered proper, but the conduct of those of Lisbon is certainly very stormy and violent. Just below the fish market is the place where the boats from the ships lying in the roadstead arrive and depart, and where the gondoliers with their gondolas wait to carry

Aboard a Dutch Troop Transport
en route to South Africa, 1802

those who wish to be taken to their ships or on the other side of the Tagus. As soon as a person nears this place, he is immediately surrounded by these people. Not one of them allows the others the opportunity to serve. A person is pulled first here and then there, occasionally lifted into the air and carried away by one of these men, until finally, the person finds himself safely in the gondola of one or the other, which brings this scene to an end, leaving the others quarreling among themselves.

Near Belem, which has already been mentioned, lies a royal castle where the prince regent stops to eat when he comes to Lisbon from Caluche, in order to visit the state council, which occurs three times each week. At that place there is a large garden which produces nothing special except beautiful laurel and myrtle hedges. Still, there is a small menagerie maintained which is barely worth seeing. Tigers, wolves, hyenas, wild boars, and several types of birds constitute the entire display.

Aboard a Dutch Troop Transport
en route to South Africa, 1802

During our stay in this roadstead, a merchant ship sailing under the Prussian flag, also lying in the roadstead, burned to the water's edge, but no one from its crew lost his life. An Algerian frigate came in, in order to obtain rigging. The commodore served a noon meal on board, attended by the Dutch Ambassador Grasveld and his wife, the Danish Ambassador Chamberlain von Warmstaedt, the Russian Ambassador, the Swedish Consul General and his wife, and many other guests. The quarterdeck was decorated with flags. Each of the two longer sides was hung with two American flags, that ahead of the cabins with the Portuguese, and that opposite with two Dutch flags. The Prussian flag formed the overhead awning. In the evening, these decorations were lit. The party remained together until late in the night.

15 September - In the morning, at eight o'clock, the anchor was raised, and toward eleven o'clock we got under sail. As the wind was unfavorable, we again lay at anchor before

Aboard a Dutch Troop Transport
en route to South Africa, 1802

Belem.

<u>16 September</u> - toward four o'clock in the morning the wind was completely favorable and we entered the ocean.

<u>17 September</u> - Two whales of a small type which the Dutch call "North Capers" came into view. These force a great amount of water through the nose, so high, and with such force, that it becomes a spray.

<u>18 September</u> - We were in the latitude of the ocean end of Gibraltar.

<u>19 September</u> - For the first time, religious services were held, and at the same time, baptism for a daughter born a few days previously to Fusilier Dovert. Lieutenant Colonel Mueller, Major von Gilten, Captain Mueller, Madam Close, Madam de Marin, and the commodore, who held the child for baptism, were the God-parents. The chaplain took his place between the two companies, on a secure block, and before him was a music stand, both of which were decorated with a blue and yellow flag, the colors of our uniforms.

Aboard a Dutch Troop Transport
en route to South Africa, 1802

The baptismal basin was formed by two, one on top of the other, drums, covered with a flag on which was a blue and white star.

<u>24 September</u> - Toward noon the commodore signaled the *Maria Reigersbergen* to sail toward the land in the southwest, and to return in the evening. Nothing was discovered. Today for the first time, we saw flying fish.

<u>25 September</u> - Toward one o'clock in the morning, a severe storm began. Thunder on the open sea, where it strikes against nothing, is completely different from that on land, not as rolling, and more similar to the heaviest guns of a battery. In order not to collide with our ship during the darkness of night, and as a result of usual sudden increased wind accompanying the storm, the *Maria Reigersbergen* moved away, and at daybreak was out of sight. At twelve o'clock noon, the ship's, Doctor Grossart, died after suffering with diarrhea for eleven days. He was 32 years old and a picture of health and strength. As it was just the time when the sailors ate their noon meal, the carpenters were

Aboard a Dutch Troop Transport
en route to South Africa, 1802

not allowed to eat until they had finished the coffin, and this situation was so effective, and speeded the work so well, that one and one-half hours after his death, the dead doctor already lay in his coffin. True, such a coffin is made without any artistic touches and is provided with a flat cover. The practice, however, of boring all sides, like a fish trap, is certainly not to be criticized, because this would be very useful in an apparent death [Scheintode]. Further, a dead person, without any difference [as to rank], is neither washed nor has his clothing changed. In order to prevent the coffin from floating on the water, 12-pound cannon balls are placed in it. During the evening, after five o'clock, the coffin was lowered overboard. It was covered twice with the Dutch flag, carried on the ship on netting by the so-called "Great Oarsmen" - eight sailors who belong to the boat crew of the ship's captain, and was followed by the commodore, all the naval officers, and our officer corps. Then the coffin was fastened on a rope, raised up in the air, and

Aboard a Dutch Troop Transport
en route to South Africa, 1802

after a sad-sounding signal, which the boatswain gave on his pipe, was lowered over the railing on the outermost side of the ship until it was about eight feet above the water. A sailor standing there cut the line with his knife, and so the coffin plunged into the ocean and disappeared from view. The dead man was then given an honor salute of nine cannon shots. Also, during the ceremony of putting the body over the side, the large flag, which is normally not flown at sea, was raised to half-mast.

26 September - During the afternoon, two swallows and two yellow water wagtails came on board, which caused us to assume that we were not far from land. At six o'clock on the morning of

27 September - We discovered the two Canary Islands, La Sanvages, which were lying just about two and one-half miles to our right.

28 September - Early in the morning the island of Tenerife came into view, and during the afternoon, the island of Grand Canary. In

Aboard a Dutch Troop Transport
en route to South Africa, 1802

the morning an owl of the screech-owl type and a cuckoo were noticed on board.

<u>29 September</u> - After two o'clock in the afternoon we arrived at the roadstead of Santa Cruz, on the island of Tenerife. As usual a Spanish boat approached us and asked if we had any contagious disease on board. Upon receiving a negative reply, a man indicated the place to anchor, which was not where we would have chosen. At three o'clock we lay at anchor. Most fortunately, and quite unexpectedly, we found all the ships belonging to our squadron were already here in the roadstead. The *Kartmaar*, which during our departure together from the roadstead at Texel, as mentioned earlier, had run aground, had painstakingly worked itself free, returned to the mentioned roadstead, and then had again gotten under sail. It had not taken a course through the Channel, but hoping to find favorable winds, sailed to the north of England, and on the 27th of this month, arrived here. On the same day, *Bato*, which we had left in the Channel, and which had lain

Aboard a Dutch Troop Transport
en route to South Africa, 1802

nine days at the roadstead at Plymouth, arrived. The *Maria Reigersbergen*, which had departed from us on the 25th, had also arrived here this morning. The captain of the *Kartmaar*, who was the senior in rank, greeted the commodore with a thirteen gun salute, whereupon the commodore fired an equal number in return. The part of the island of Tenerife in sight in this area forms an inward turning arch, in the middle of which lies Santa Cruz. On both sides of the city a row of mountains is to be seen along the ocean, the climbing of which, during our present stay, required one and one-half hours. Beyond the city the land rises gently, then more rapidly, then more steeply, until it nearly attains the height of the noted mountains, so that, in this manner, an open kettle is formed. This region, as well as the foot of every mountain, has been made into orchards such as are seldom encountered. On the upper reaches of the mountains, which are here and there cut through by steep ravines, a view of the more distant forest-covered

Aboard a Dutch Troop Transport
en route to South Africa, 1802

mountains is provided. One sees vineyards and the houses of the vintners. Further, a large part of the mountains is covered with wild fig trees, and the upper areas are covered primarily with lava and volcanic rock. The region and the city have, as far as can be seen, an exceptionally dead and decayed appearance, which certainly the present season, when the local rainy season is very near, might contribute, although nothing enlivens it. Except for six or seven palm trees, nothing else of this type is to be seen. No birds are to be seen, even in the mountains, and even the sea-swallows are seldom seen. The mountains are seldom without fog, now. First it covers to the foot, then the middle can be seen, and then the peaks are unveiled, forming all possible figures, and so the view thereof often changes very drastically and pleasantly within a short time.

Santa Cruz is the size of a small country city. The streets are narrow, but well-paved and rather clean. The houses, without exception, are white plaster; all have flat roofs, a few are

Aboard a Dutch Troop Transport
en route to South Africa, 1802

pleasant to view. For the most part they are only one story high. On both ends of the city, toward the roadstead, lie forts consisting of brickwork. In the vicinity of the larger one, which stands on the right, Admiral Neber, during an unsuccessful landing attempt at the sound below, lost his arm, and the same ball killed his adjutant and also another individual. To the right and left of the city, other small forts are to be seen.

Aboard a Dutch Troop Transport
en route to South Africa, 1802

10

The governor of all the Canary Islands has his residence here. The present governor is Don Joseph Periac, a man about 70 years old. He offered the squadron all possible help and showed himself to be very friendly. Only a limited amount of water is brought to the city through a conduit, and a part of the water goes to a fountain in the garden of the governor. Commissary General de Mitt, who visited the governor, remarked that this fountain was not in operation, and received this reply, "I have ordered the fountain is not to flow while my friends the Hollanders are here, so that they can more quickly be provided the necessary water." A Spanish soldier stole a Dutch guilder from one of our jaegers. After three days the thief was sentenced to eight years in prison. The local residents are very polite. Those of the lower classes are poorly dressed, but as a rule, the ordinary women and girls wear a large piece of thin white woolen cloth on their head, which also hangs down over the shoulders and

Aboard a Dutch Troop Transport
en route to South Africa, 1802

back, to the calf, as a coat, and on top of this a felt hat. An ordinary inn is sought in vain; a hard boiled egg is difficult to obtain, even for much money. Many of the squadron who went on land received absolutely nothing. To be sure, there are residents who understand the need to serve strangers, but they must be spoken with early enough, in order to meet the obligation, and even so, the food is bad and must be paid for at the highest prices. The common animals which are used for traveling and pulling loads are mules, donkeys, and dromedaries. It is customary here to carry a corpse in an open coffin to the grave. In this manner, a Spanish officer was carried. In the van, about twenty well-fed monks trotted, then came the corpse dressed in full uniform, and only then, the usual procession.

The ocean in the local bay is always very high, and the breakers are so powerful that even during calm weather, they beat 25 to 30 feet up on the rocks and cliffs. During the still of the night, a person believes he is hearing the

Aboard a Dutch Troop Transport
en route to South Africa, 1802

howling of the tide rising above and crashing over the rocks. Ships which have to halt here for a lengthy period of time put out eight anchors, because by the strong onshore southwest winds, so much water is driven into the bay that, even with this precaution, anchors are frequently torn loose. No Spanish warship is stationed here, but a small merchant ship manned by four sailors serves as the watch ship. From the roadstead in clear weather, the island of Grand Canary and the peak of the familiar mountain, Pico, on the island of Tenerife, can be seen.

30 September - Our ship had a leak for some time, through which in a calm sea, during one week (in four hours) about three inches of water entered, but when the ship had to sail against the waves, the amount of water which entered increased. The commodore, therefore, by means of a signal, called all the carpenters of the squadron on board to find this leak and close it. The officer who received this order misread the signal, and unfortunately gave an

Aboard a Dutch Troop Transport
en route to South Africa, 1802

order resulting in all doctors of the squadron being called on board. These gentlemen immediately determined, however, that the problem was not to be corrected through medical or surgical means. Therefore, they were sent back and this time, the carpenters were called.

<u>6 October</u> - A sailor who died of dysentery, because it is forbidden to put a corpse overboard, in the roadstead, but must be buried on land, was buried late this evening without ceremony.

<u>8 October</u> - At eight o'clock in the morning, the squadron raised the first anchor. This made most of the inhabitants of Santa Cruz very happy, because during our stay here the prices of foodstuffs had climbed so much that they were not sure how much longer they could survive. Toward one o'clock, the second anchor was raised, and at two o'clock we again got under sail. Sunset made a beautiful view. The island which we left was completely covered with clouds. Only the peak of Pico

Aboard a Dutch Troop Transport
en route to South Africa, 1802

reached an unbelievable height above them and appeared to be a small round hill. At the very top a small gold-colored cloud hung.

9 October - During the morning, Pico was visible from the foot to the peak; only at about the middle, there was a small white cloud. Toward noon it again disappeared in the clouds.

11 October - To provide for the health of the non-commissioned officers and privates, Lieutenant Colonel Mueller had purchased a large quantity of the local wine at Santa Cruz, and from today on, except on Sundays and Thursdays, on which days cognac is served, a portion of about one-third of a pint will be issued daily at eleven o'clock. The total cost of the wine was charged to those receiving it. Also, the sailors received a like portion of wine, for which the baptismal money, put in at the Barlings, was applied.

13 October - Toward evening, a flying fish entered in between decks. It had the color and appearance of a medium size herring. Its length, not counting an inch long tail fin, was

Aboard a Dutch Troop Transport
en route to South Africa, 1802

about five inches. A half inch behind the head were the two and one-half inch wings of a thin skin. The flying fish were often followed by porpoise. [The word in the manuscript is Hakenrochen, which may mean hake, but porpoise seems to fit the rest of the sentence.] which were mentioned earlier, so that by the hundreds they flew from the water, in all directions, for twenty or thirty paces, and finally fell down. In this way, many were caught when flying from one of the following porpoise, or if he fortunately escaped, because he again fell, became the prize of another, which found itself in the region, because these porpoise, also are found in an abundance during the chase.

<u>12 October</u> [sic] - Early in the morning we passed the Tropic of Cancer.

<u>16 October</u> - The *Bato*, despite putting on all possible sail, could not keep up with the other ships. On the other hand, these frequently found it necessary to lay to and wait for the *Bato*. However, as a ship by frequently halting

Aboard a Dutch Troop Transport
en route to South Africa, 1802

and laying to can suffer and easily develop leaks due to the force of the waves which it no longer cuts through, and also because the *Maria Reigersbergen*, due to a shortage of space, had only been able to take on enough water for nine weeks, therefore, the commodore, with the concurrence of the captains of the *Kartmaar* and the *Maria Reigersbergen*, who had been called on board for this reason, decided to leave *Bato*- which was given the news of the decision.

17 October - Religious services were held.

18 October - Early in the morning the *Bato* was out of sight.

20 October - Due to contrary winds our course could not be held, which surprised the seamen all the more, as they were otherwise accustomed at this latitude to have a wind which generally held steadily from Tenerife to the sixth or eighth degree of north latitude, without much variation, so that the setting of the sails often remained the same for days. By this means the ship hastened its voyage, which

Aboard a Dutch Troop Transport
en route to South Africa, 1802

it generally lost in a calm after crossing the Equator. Toward evening the Isle of May, which remained lying on our right, was seen.

21 October - At sunset, the island of Santiago came into view.

25 October - The commodore had heard that today was the birthday of our prince, and therefore gave the squadron the signal to raise our flag.

27 October - In the morning we saw a Danish ship ahead of us. There are often sharks near the ship, but at noon today, there was an exceptionally large one which remained near us for hours, but which could not be caught. Therefore, I had the opportunity to study the small fish which are always in large numbers near the sharks, and, as there is a belief that they guide the sharks, they are called boatmen by the sailors. They are three inches long, dark and light blue, which colors alternate pleasantly, and they have the exact shape of a grundel [a type of fish], which I could clearly see in one of them that was caught. They stay

Aboard a Dutch Troop Transport
en route to South Africa, 1802

very close to the sharks, often staying to the rear of a shark when it was frightened by something and, of its own accord, turned and went in another direction without being led. Often several boatmen fish would move ahead of the shark and it would suddenly turn without taking them into account, so that they would have to hurry after it. It is therefore quite obvious that these little fish are not the leaders of the sharks, but that they find nourishment on the rough, outer skin.

28 October - A French ship was in sight.

30 October - Three ships were holding the same course with us. One had already been seen yesterday; the other two were Spanish.

31 October - The two Spanish ships which had come into view yesterday approached us and asked for the position observation we had made today.

3 November - A French and a Portuguese ship were discovered ahead of us.

4 November - The Portuguese ship was constantly in sight. In the vicinity of the

Aboard a Dutch Troop Transport
en route to South Africa, 1802

Equator it often rains and very heavily, but such a rain is never persistent and lasts not more than a few hours, usually only an hour or less. It is more like a cloudburst than like an ordinary rain. Rain clouds often come with a strong, swirling wind, so that a ship can easily be sunk in only a moment. For this reason, as soon as such a cloud is seen, everyone must hurry to his post, and every measure is taken to ensure the security of the ship. The sailors take positions so that they have the correct line in hand and only await the signal to carry out the necessary maneuvers. In this manner, favorable, approaching, strong winds are welcome because the winds near the Equator are otherwise generally weak, and often, for several weeks, only calm weather is encountered, and now and then the ship even losses ground. Therefore, it can happen, and we encountered this situation ourselves a few days ago, that a ship on the same course as ours, with the help of such an approaching rain cloud, ran some distance ahead of us with full

Aboard a Dutch Troop Transport
en route to South Africa, 1802

sails, while we were in a complete calm and did not advance the least distance. Every effort is made aboard ship to catch the rainwater, in part to increase that on hand, in part also because, when it is boiled, by which means it loses the taken-in taste of the rigging and woodwork, it tastes much better than the water found on board. At noon today, for example, so much rain fell in twenty minutes that 533 gallons [64 Anker - an Anker equals eight and one-third gallons] of water were caught just on the quarterdeck, a flat surface of 672 square feet. The diligence with which soldiers and sailors, by such an opportunity, seek in other parts of the ship and by all means, to catch water and to use it, for all purposes, is unbelievable. Some catch it to drink; others undress down to their trousers and use the rain for bathing; and still others wash their shirts and socks with it. Aboard ship one must be satisfied for a long time with a small portion of stinking water, with which he would hardly dirty a glass on land, and learn to treasure the good fortune of

Aboard a Dutch Troop Transport
en route to South Africa, 1802

having healthy and clean water. Still, every stinking drop of water in such a situation is sought out and gladly taken.

5 November - At the noon position sighting today, we learned that because of a contrary wind since yesterday, we had been blown backward fourteen miles.

9 November - Since October 20, we have had either calm or contrary winds, which made holding the course, difficult, and only seldom was the wind favorable. This caused a general discontent. Finally, at noon today, a welcome, favorable, and long wished-for wind arose.

10 November - The wind became a full southeast trade wind, which brought joy and high spirits once again on board ship.

14 November - About four o'clock in the morning we crossed the Equator. Yesterday the wind was very strong, The ship cut through the seas with such force that the water frequently washed over the fore part of the ship. The knowledge that such speed brings us nearer the goal of our voyage creates an indescribably

Aboard a Dutch Troop Transport
en route to South Africa, 1802

pleasant atmosphere and arouses a cheerful mood.

15 November - The thermometer showed the temperature of the air, in the shade, to be 28 degrees [Celcius], and that the interior of the ship was much warmer. The thermometer in the powder room read 98 degrees. [Fahrenheit? ---Possibly the first reading was a copying error.] Although the sailors working there had stripped down to their trousers, they were barely in a condition to perform their work. An English ship was in view.

Aboard a Dutch Troop Transport
en route to South Africa, 1802

11

<u>29 November</u> - By the opportunity, when two brothers, eleven and thirteen years old, serving as cabin boys, were accused by the ship's doctor of having stolen pastries, we saw an example of nautical barbarity. The complaint could not be proven; also, the pastries could have been taken by only one of the accused. Therefore, it was determined that the dark act would be decided in a manner practiced in ancient times, the so-called divine judgment. The two brothers were separated by means of a barrel hoop, which was fastened behind them so that neither, by getting too close to the other, could avoid the lashes which they would give one another with a piece of line, and thus might make himself less exposed. Then they were told that they were to beat on the other until the guilty one would admit his crime, with the further admonition, that the one who tried to protect the other, would receive severe lashes from the quarter-master, who was already standing there. The younger of the two brothers

Aboard a Dutch Troop Transport
en route to South Africa, 1802

began to accuse his brother and proclaimed his innocence in the most moving expressions. The older trembled with his entire body in pity for his brother, but had to commence whipping him, at which the younger was ordered to do likewise and not to let up. But, because the greater pain caused him to cease, he received as ordered, from the quartermaster present, the most miserable beating. Nearly all the naval officers were present at this theater, and could not laugh enough at the action

<u>21 November</u> - Religious services were held.

<u>22 November</u> - Commencing today the non-commissioned officers and upward, will receive wine only three times each week. Today we are under the eighteenth degree of south latitude, and for the first time saw the so-called Cape clouds, which show themselves during the evening under a bright sky, west of the Milky Way. Actually there are three, two of which have a bluish-white color and have the mentioned position, while the third, which has a bluish-blue appearance, is seen in the Milky Way. The latter, which can only be seen by a

Aboard a Dutch Troop Transport
en route to South Africa, 1802

completely clear sky, was not visible today. They appear like small clouds, but consist in reality of many stars and are visible as far as the Cape [of Good Hope] and further. By the for some time constantly favorable winds, we have often traveled more than two degrees in 24 hours, so that the lengthening of daylight, which amounts to four minutes for every degree is very noticeable. During the shortening of the daylight, this was not noticeable, because we then made only small advances.

<u>26 November</u> - In the forenoon we crossed the Tropic of Capricorn. The stars here appear to have an astonishing brightness, and the evening star shows itself to be unusually large and with a sparkling shine.

<u>29 November</u> - Commencing today the non-commissioned officers and upward, receive only half of their previous portion of cheese, and the other half is to be made up with olive oil. Our people do not like it, but accept it. On the other hand the sailors enjoy eating it with zwieback, and also use it to flavor their peas.

<u>1 December</u> - A ship's soldier, who died of

Aboard a Dutch Troop Transport
en route to South Africa, 1802

scurvy, was buried at sea, and this loss was replaced when the wife of Surgeon Mueller gave birth; at least the number of souls on board remained the same. For some days the scurvy has been increasing among our troops, also. Its symptoms are rot in the gums, swollen knees, and brown spots on the shin bones, which turn black, and enlarge until they merge together.

2 December - The wind which has been so favorable became variable. More than one hundred dolphins approached very near to our ship and spent several hours playing about. They are twelve to fourteen feet long and of a black-brown color. The head is about one and one-half feet thick, is bluntly rounded, and has a very indeterminate shape. Close behind the head is an opening about two inches in diameter through which water is often forced into the air with a noise. On the end of the tail, which is rounded and tapers down to about two inches, there is a crossways fin. Another is in about the middle of the back, slightly more toward the head, and has the shape of a

Aboard a Dutch Troop Transport
en route to South Africa, 1802

right triangle whose hypotenuse, of abot sixteen inches, is toward the head. There are fins on both sides of the head, about one foot long and three inches wide, which narrow to a point. One of these dolphins was shot with a rifle, causing a large surrounding area to be colored by the blood from the wound, but no dead dolphin came to the surface, although a stream of blood from the head wound could be seen rising from one.

4 December - During the evening, Corporal [Matthias] Beck of the Jaeger Company, who had died of old age during the afternoon, was buried at sea. The custom aboard ship in burying an individual who was not an officer is as follows. As soon as someone dies, he is laid out briefly on the fore part of the ship, and then sewn into his hammock, in which his mattress and blankets remain, and in which four cannonballs are laid at his feet by the sailmaker. Sunset is the usual time when the dead are buried, barring any circumstances such as evidence of contagious disease. The deceased is laid on a plank especially for this

Aboard a Dutch Troop Transport
en route to South Africa, 1802

purpose. The cabin or messmates with whom he served carry the board, through an opening made by the assembled crew, to the side of the foremast and set it there, from whence it is then lifted into the air on the command of the sailing master, "one, two, in God's name," then swung out and dropped into the sea. After this takes place, the pallbearers are given a drink of cognac. Officers and non-commissioned officers are lowered over the side of the ship near the region where Corporal Beck died, uttered the death curse which was noted for its originality by the entire ship's crew. He wished that the one who hoped to become a corporal due to Beck's death would be driven so deeply into the sea by a lighting bolt, that he could command Beck to halt.

5 December - Religious services were held, at which time the first born child of Surgeon Mueller was baptized.

6 December - From today on, everyone, without regard to rank, had his water ration reduced by one-seventh part, which

Aboard a Dutch Troop Transport
en route to South Africa, 1802

precautionary measure was necessary, because of the inconsistency of the wind, and the even more uncertainty of the time of our arrival at our destination, although our ship was provided with 220 casks [Leggers], each holding 132 gallons, and totaling 5,120 Anker [sic - about 30,000] gallons of water upon departing from Holland and having taken on board an equal amount at Lisbon and also at Santa Cruz. With the greatest possible economy, the daily water ration amounted to three half casks, about 470 gallons [56 Anker]. [There are apparently copying errors.]

    7 December - Fusilier [Henrich] Stempelmann, who died of an apoplectic stroke this morning, was buried at sea. It was noted that he was the one who had brought Corporal Beck, who died three days ago, into the battalion as a recruit.

    8 December - By a southwest wind and a temperature of 64 degrees, we find ourselves at 31^0 south latitude. Here is such a penetrating cold, or more to the point, so much cold, after having been accustomed to the greater warmth,

Aboard a Dutch Troop Transport
en route to South Africa, 1802

that when the crew is commanded to work on deck, they wrap up in blankets and look for their jackets and winter vests.

<u>10 December</u> - At a temperature of 20 degrees the air is raw and unpleasant. The sunshine which one avoided a few days ago is now diligently sought, and it feels as good as sunshine in springtime.

<u>13 December</u> - With the help of a very favorable and constant wind, at noon today, we had traveled 52 and one-half miles in the last 24 hours. Once during this period we sailed only 10 and one-half miles in a week. During the entire voyage not one day of sailing (from one noon to the next) was so favorable, and in general all the ship's personnel were filled with joy.

<u>14 December</u> - This morning, as a result of consumption, Jaeger [Daniel] Graebe [or Grebe], born in Heringhausen, died and was buried at sea at sunset.

<u>16 December</u> - A so-called Cape-dove was seen. It belongs to the plentiful order of gulls of the size and shape and flight, similar to the

Aboard a Dutch Troop Transport
en route to South Africa, 1802

dove, and prefers to stay near land, which according to our reckoning can only be at a distance of about sixty miles.

<u>17 December</u> - During the morning, Fusilier [Christian] Konig of the 4th Company and born in Korbach, who died yesterday evening of consumption, complicated by scurvy, was buried at sea. A great many sea birds of all types, including among others, Cape doves, were seen.

<u>18 December</u> - Early this morning, considerable Cape trumpets, a kind of reed four or more feet long, were discovered. A tone similar to the shawn tones [The shawn is an obsolete wood-wind instrument with a double reed.] can be produced by blowing through them, and they are found along every ocean coast.

Aboard a Dutch Troop Transport
en route to South Africa, 1802

12

At eleven o'clock the coast could be seen clearly without a telescope, and the Tafelberg was completely visible. The word "Land!" was the only one heard for a long time aboard ship, after land was discovered. There was not room enough on deck for all of those who came up from within the ship to see the so long wished-for sight. The sick recovered their strength, left their hammocks, and with effort pulled themselves up from below deck, and others so weak to do so, were supported by their comrades. With a handshake men wished one another good luck for having survived the long trip and having attained their destination. At two o'clock, the cliffs and other features could be clearly differentiated. At three-thirty, we turned left in order to run along the Tafelberg, whereby, as we were near the coast, from which we were only about a half mile, we lost our favorable wind and encountered instead, a calm. Also, this short distance from the coast caused an unusual change in the temperature readings.

Aboard a Dutch Troop Transport
en route to South Africa, 1802

During the morning it was 64 degrees, and at noon, 68 degrees. The temperature then climbed between three-thirty and four o'clock to 23 degrees [Celsius ? - 73 degrees Fahrenheit ?], and between four and four-thirty, to 75 degrees. It remained this high until five o'clock, and then fell by sunset to 67 degrees. Toward evening, a weak but favorable wind arose, which allowed us to approach nearer to the roadstead. By the so-called Society House, an inn at a distance of about an hour before Capetown, a great many people were to be seen already assembled, as well as those hurrying there with wagons, on horseback, and on foot, in order to watch our squadron enter. At nine o'clock, the English harbor captain came on board by us to make the customary inspection of the squadron, and then visited the other ships, also. At eleven-thirty we lay at anchor in the Tafelberg, at a distance of about a mile from Capetown.

19 December - The joy of the final successful and fortunate arrival at the place of our destination afforded an entire night of little,

Aboard a Dutch Troop Transport
en route to South Africa, 1802

or even no sleep, and already at four o'clock in the morning, the deck was crowded with those curious ones wanting to catch a view of the capital of their future residence, which they had been unable to see upon their arrival in the roadstead, because of darkness. The view was improved by the exceptionally bright and clear sunrise, which improved the already existing cheerful mood considerably. At five o'clock the British Vice Admiral Reger [Roger?]-Curtis, lying in the roadstead with thirteen large and small warships, greeted the commodore with a fifteen gun salute, which was returned by the commodore with an equal number. Then the fort greeted the commodore with an equal number of shots. At five-thirty the English vice admiral sent his flag captain to congratulate the commodore on his fortunate arrival, and at the same time, to inform the commodore that he would give his congratulations in person at ten o'clock. A great many people came in boats from the city in order to seek and welcome relatives and friends or to get news, either written or oral, of those who had remained

Aboard a Dutch Troop Transport
en route to South Africa, 1802

behind. Fresh butter, bread, eggs, vegetables, fruit, and such, in abundance, were brought on board, and with the enjoyment of these articles, which we had gone without for so long, we overcame, at least, the clarity of memory of the hardships endured during our voyage. At eight o'clock, the commodore answered the forts greeting with fifteen shots, also. At ten o'clock the English admiral made his scheduled visit to the commodore. His boat, on which flew the admiral's red flag, was followed by eleven others with long pennants, at a ship's length, one behind the other, according to their rank. All the officers were in full dress uniform and all the sailors manning the oars were dressed in white. The whole line provided a splendid view and returned [to their fleet] in the same order, whereupon the English admiral, after the last boat of the procession left our ship, received a fifteen gun salute.

20 December - At eleven o'clock the commodore, accompanied by the captains of the *Kartmaar* and the *Maria Reigersbergen*, in special boats, made his return visit to the

Aboard a Dutch Troop Transport
en route to South Africa, 1802

English admiral, and upon his departure also received a fifteen gun salute. During the evening such a strong southeast wind arose that we feared we would be torn from our anchors.

<u>21 December</u> - The debarkation of the troops had been firmly fixed for today, and Admiral Curtis had offered a number of boats from his fleet to expedite the action. Since, however, the strong winds which arose yesterday had not slackened, no one believed that the English boats would come. However, the offered boats were actually present at our ship at five o'clock in the morning, and under full sail, not being rowed, despite the constant forceful movement of the water, which required the exertion of all their effort to hold fast, until they could take on their cargo. The debarkation of part of the battalion which was on the *Pluto*, except for a few men left behind with the baggage, was successfully completed, although in so doing, some boats, in danger of sinking, barely escaped. Some of these beat against other ships lying in the roadstead, others beat against the cliffs present about a half mile below the

Aboard a Dutch Troop Transport
en route to South Africa, 1802

designated landing place, and arrived with noticeable damage, on land. Several of the earliest departed boats did not reach the landing place until late in the afternoon. I found myself with some troops in a boat commanded by an English sea cadet. It was nearly steered into an anchor cable of a merchant ship, from which, in a collision, we could not have been saved. The danger was so apparent that the sailors on the mentioned ship were already standing with lines ready to throw to us as a means of rescue. The speed with which the sail was struck and above all, the activity of the sailors, tore us from the present misfortune, drove us from the side of the ship, and we then resumed our voyage. We arrived on land, thoroughly soaked, after being on the water for more than two hours, during which time the water which fell into the boat from a number of causes, and from the waves beating over us, had thoroughly drenched us. Because of the strength of the wind, Admiral Curtis gave his boats a signal, at noon, to discontinue the debarkation of the troops. Several months before the departure of our

Aboard a Dutch Troop Transport
en route to South Africa, 1802

squadron, the Dutch government had sent out Captain Benn of the 9th Jaeger Battalion, who had been designated director of the hospital, and Doctor Dibbetz and Herr Mueller to prepare for the reception of the troops and other necessary arrangements. As a result, everything pertaining thereto, was found in the best condition. The troops received their quarters in a very large building not far from the fort. This building had been built by the Dutch East Indies Company as a hospital, and was now fully functional as a military barracks. The proper care of the sick was well tended to in a wing of the mentioned building, separated from the main building and adjacent to the hospital. It was completely adopted to the reception of the sick. The officers, meanwhile, were quartered with the residents of the city, by which means I had one of the best quarters I ever had, in the home of Herr Anos, one of the most respected local business men, from whom I received exceptional courtesy, as well as from his family. In addition to their previous pay, and from now on, the troops, from non-commissioned officers

Aboard a Dutch Troop Transport
en route to South Africa, 1802

downward, received daily without suffering a cash withholding, one and one-half pounds of bread, three-fourths pound of meat, and some vegetables, and weekly, seventeen and one-half pounds of wood and a half pound of candles.

23 December - The landing from the *Kartmaar* and the *Maria Reigersbergen*, which had been interrupted by the strong southeast wind, was completed today. In the afternoon, the *Bato* likewise arrived at the local roadstead.

24 December - Commissary General de Mitt and Governor Jansens came on land with the greeting of a 21 gun salute from the fort, and were received by the English Governor General Dunkas. The latter had sent a wagon for the commissary general and the governor, which however, was not used because the mentioned officers proceeded on foot to the so-called Company Garden, with an English cavalry escort. General Dunkas had his quarters there. The road leading in was manned on both sides by English troops, who extended the usual honors. General Dunkas had assembled many of his officers around him, also, and received

Aboard a Dutch Troop Transport
en route to South Africa, 1802

those approaching with attention to the usual ceremonies for such an occasion. After the commissary general himself had read his credentials, received from the Dutch government, and both sides had attested to their friendly conduct, the commissary general and the governor with their accompaniment returned to the fort in which they made their residence, and which for that reason, already for some time, had been vacated by General Dunkas. The throng of curious which came hurrying to see their future governor was very great. General Dunkas gave the commissary general and the governor a splendid noon meal, at which the health of the King of England and the Dutch government was toasted, and each time a 21 gun salute was fired by two artillery pieces brought there especially for this purpose.

25 December - The officers' visit to General Dunkas and Vice Admiral Curtis was conducted under the leadership of Colonel Henry, commandant of the Dutch troops stationed in this colony. A long sea voyage was completed in such good condition, despite the

Aboard a Dutch Troop Transport
en route to South Africa, 1802

unpleasantness which we have certainly had during our trip here from Europe, and in good measure, but no real misfortune overcame us. A great many insignificant things, such as the scarcity of milk, no rich butter, nor any vegetables, except for dried peas and beans and such, must be taken into account, also the situation required drinking completely foul water, which on such a trip can not be avoided, and we could not forget the preparation of bad food and the continuously exceptional unseemliness. Meat was put before us, but overwhelming proof of its rottenness easily forgiven, although frequently its pestilential smell caused the entire group at the table to curse. For the moment, this has been put aside. The bread also became unpleasant, although the mixture during the leavening of the dough retained its taste, but the best appetite could not eat it. But nothing could make the continuance of our life doubtful. We crossed the Equator at a time when the sun was on its way to the other hemisphere, and the heat was very tolerable, and further, in that area, we were not delayed by

Aboard a Dutch Troop Transport
en route to South Africa, 1802

wind calm, which is generally the case. We were favored by an advantageous and completely unexpected wind. Also, we remained free of contagious disease, and the loss, which the battalion suffered during the voyage, through deaths, consisted of a sergeant, a corporal, a jaeger, and three fusiliers, including Sergeant [Theodor] Kneuper [or Neuper] of the 6th Company and Fusilier [Henrich] Zuekkert, [or Luekkeert] of the 5th Company, both of whom died on the *Kartmaar*. Nearly all of these men, prior to their deaths, had been threatened for some time by the approach of death.

The following table shows how far the ship *Pluto*, during that part of the voyage from Tenerife to the Cape, traveled daily, from one noon to the next, based on latitude and the degree of Fahrenheit shown on the thermometer in the shade, mornings, noon, and evenings. The south latitude under which the Tafelberg lies is 23 degrees 55 minutes. [The table was not included in my German copy.]

Aboard a Dutch Troop Transport
en route to South Africa, 1802

Copied in Stuttgart in December 1931 from the diary which is in the possession of the writer in Ludwigsburg, by Hilmar Gieseken Stoecker, Archeological student.

This is the Translator

Howard Horne, Past PresidentGeneral of the National Society of Sons of the American Revolution, presented the Society's Gold Good Citizenship Award to the author at a Dover, Delaware meeting on 8 April 2006. Dr. Marie Burgoyne attended the meeting with her husband.

The translator, Bruce E. Burgoyne, was born 25 October 1924 in Benton Harbor, Michigan, and is married with three grown sons. His wife Marie, a Doctor of Education from the University of Southern California, is a helpful research companion and source of encouragement. Mr. Burgoyne's education includes a Master of Arts in Social Science (History, Economics, and Government) from Trinity University in San Antonio, Texas, plus course work at half a dozen other colleges and universities in America and overseas. He has also completed numerous military courses in such subjects as German language, Counterintelligence, and Public Information.

This is the Translator

His employment, in addition to recent teaching assignments at Delaware State College and Immaculata College, include twenty years in the military with service in the Navy, Army, and Air Force, and six years working for the Army as a civilian Intelligence officer. During his military and civilian service he lived more than six years in Germany, during which time he attended German Language School in Oberammergau, two months of in-depth Belitz type language training, living in a German household, and interviewing and interrogating in German of persons of intelligence and counterintelligence interest.

Mr. Burgoyne's forty plus years of researching the role of the Hessians in the American Revolutionary War, include visiting archives in England and Holland as well as archives in the United States and Germany. His research has resulted in the translation and publication of more than thirty-five major Hessian documents.

Other Heritage Books by Bruce E. Burgoyne:

Aboard a Dutch Troop Transport: A Diary Written by Captain Ludwig Alberti of the Waldeck 5th Battalion

A Hessian Officer's Diary of the American Revolution Translated from an Anonymous Ansbach-Bayreuth Diary and the Prechtel Diary

Canada During the American Revolutionary War: Lieutenant Friedrich Julius von Papet's Journal of the Sea Voyage to North America and the Campaign Conducted There

CD: A Hessian Diary of the American Revolution

CD: A Hessian Officer's Diary of The American Revolution

CD: A Hessian Report on the People, the Land, the War of Eighteenth Century America, as Noted in the Diary of Chaplain Philipp Waldeck, 1776-1780

CD: Ansbach-Bayreuth Diaries from the Revolutionary War

CD: Canada During the America Revolutionary War

CD: Diaries of Two Ansbach Jaegers

CD: The Hessian Collection, Volume 1: Revolutionary War Era

CD: They Also Served. Women with the Hessian Auxiliaries

CD: Waldeck Soldiers of the American Revolutionary War

Defeat, Disaster, and Dedication

Diaries of Two Ansbach Jaegers

Eighteenth Century America (A Hessian Report on the People, the Land, the War) as Noted in the Diary of Chaplain Philipp Waldeck (1776-1780)

Enemy Views: The American Revolutionary War as Recorded by the Hessian Participants

English Army and Navy Lists Compiled During the American Revolutionary War by Ansbach-Bayreuth Lieutenant Johann Ernst Prechtel

Georg Pausch's Journal and Reports of the Campaign in America, as Translated from the German Manuscript in the Lidgerwood Collection in the Morristown Historical Park Archives, Morristown, New Jersey

Hesse-Hanau Order Books, a Diary and Roster: A Collection of Items Concerning the Hesse-Hanau Contingent of "Hessians" Fighting Against the American Colonists in the Revolutionary War

Hessian Chaplains: Their Diaries and Duties

Hessian Letters and Journals and a Memoir

Journal of a Hessian Grenadier Battalion

Journal of the Hesse-Cassel Jaeger Corps

Journal of the Prince Charles Regiment
Translated by Bruce E. Burgoyne; Edited by Dr. Marie E. Burgoyne

Most Illustrious Hereditary Prince: Letters to Their Prince from Members of Hesse-Hanau Military Contingent in the Service of England During the American Revolution

Notes from a British Museum

Order Book of the Hesse-Cassel von Mirbach Regiment

Revolutionary War Letters Written by Hessian Officers: Generals Wilhelm von Knyphausen, Carl Wilhelm Von Hachenberg, Friedrich Wilhelm von Lossberg, Johann Friedrich Cochenhausen, Friedrich Von Riedesel and Major Carl Leopold von Baurmeister
Bruce E. Burgoyne and Dr. Marie E. Burgoyne

The Diary of Lieutenant von Bardeleben and Other von Donop Regiment

The Hesse-Cassel Mirbach Regiment in the American Revolution

These Were the Hessians

The Third English-Waldeck Regiment in the American Revolutionary War

The Trenton Commanders: Johann Gottlieb Rall and George Washington, as Noted in Hessian Diaries

Waldeck Soldiers of the American Revolutionary War

www.ingramcontent.com/pod-product-compliance
Lightning Source LLC
Chambersburg PA
CBHW070456090426
42735CB00012B/2579